W9-AKT-540

To Karl

God Bless

Pastor Bob

I Cor. 13

THE JOURNEY TO

wholeness
& HOLINESS

FASTING AND PRAYING

2-27-08

Karl,

Stay strong ... Continue to

be a beacon!

Mike Jones

Micah 6:8

THE JOURNEY TO

wholeness

& HOLINESS

FASTING AND PRAYING

ROBERT F. LOGGINS, SR.

SECOND EDITION REVISED

H   PUBLISHED BY *Hesed Communications*

The Journey To Wholeness & Holiness

THE JOURNEY TO WHOLENESS & HOLINESS
Revised 2nd Edition: Copyright © by Robert F. Loggins 2007

Copyright © by Robert F. Loggins 2006
All rights reserved.

No part of this publication may be reproduced, stored in a retrieval system, or transmitted in any form or by any means, electronic, mechanical, photocopying, recording, or otherwise, without the prior permission of the author.

Hesed Communications, Robert F. Loggins, 15197 Eagle Chase Court Chesterfield, Missouri 63017

Cover Designed: Kristy Buchanan, Graphic Design Artist.

Printed in the United States of America
ISBN: 978-0-9797899-8-4

Unless otherwise indicated, all Scripture quotations are taken from the *King James Version* of the *Holy Bible* or are the author's revision of that version.

Verses marked NIV are taken from the *Holy Bible*, the *New International Version*, copyright © 1973, 1978, 1984 by the International Bible Society. Used by permission of Zondervan. All rights reserved.

Verses marked NLT are taken from the *Holy Bible*, the *New Living Translation*, copyright © 1996. Used by permission of Tyndale House Publishers, Inc., Wheaton, IL 60189 USA. All rights reserved.

Verses marked TNIV are taken from the *Holy Bible*, the *Today's New International Version*, copyright © 2001, 2005 by International Bible Society.

Verses marked are taken from *The Message*, copyright © 1993, 1994, 1995, 1996, 2000, 2001, 2002 by Eugene H. Peterson.

Scripture quotations marked HCSB are taken from the Holman Christian Standard Bible®, copyright © 1999, 2000, 2002, 2003 by Holman Bible Publishers. Used by permission of Holman Christian Standard Bible®, Holman CSB®, and HCSB® are federally registered trademarks of Holman Bible Publishers

The Journey To Wholeness & Holiness

To my beautiful and loving wife, Cassandra,
our sons, Beau and Jordan, and
our wonderful and compassionate church family.
You have loved me in all my seasons: winter, spring, summer and fall.
The journey has been an experience to celebrate.

To Cynthia Biehle, one of the most gifted professionals that
I have ever worked with in my writing ministry.
Her keen eye provided clarity and homogeny to the heart
and soul of The Journey To Wholeness & Holiness.

Special Acknowledgment: To five God-given ladies in my life.
The first lady is my mother, Mrs. Gladys Louise Taylor Loggins.
The second lady is my aunt, Mrs. Minnie Lee Holloway.
The third lady is my wife's grandmother, Mrs. Eula Mae Burwell.
The fourth lady is my wife's mother, Mrs. Bobbye Riley.
And the fifth and final lady is my wife, Mrs. Cassandra G. Loggins.

THE JOURNEY TO

wholeness
& HOLINESS

FASTING AND PRAYING

TABLE OF CONTENTS

THE JOURNEY TO

wholeness
& HOLINESS

FASTING AND PRAYING

Cassandra's Journey

Twenty-nine years ago, I started on a journey with my husband when we wed in a little church in my hometown of Meridian, Mississippi. Since then, my life has seen a series of phenomenal changes. These changes came from more than just getting married to a wonderful husband and starting a family; these phenomenal changes, better known as blessings, came from my personal journey to wholeness and holiness.

This book may be the culmination of my husband's life experiences, but it is so much greater than just his personal reflections. In these pages you can expect to find the keys to a closer intimacy with Christ, a deeper fullness in your life, and a renewed sense of purpose.

I know this, because I have seen these principles transform the lives of individuals in our congregation, at The WORD Is Alive Ministries, and also in the lives of our two sons, Beau and Jordan. Many of our members have approached me with stories about how their marriages have been made better, their job performance has increased, and their families have been made whole. In fact, in my own house, I have seen radical changes. While my two sons are not perfect, I have seen them both strive to practice the life changing disciplines that are written in *The Journey To Wholeness & Holiness.*

Do you desire true intimacy with God? If you do, then I can testify through personal experience, that this book can present you with the keys to unlock new and explosive blessings in your life. God has met me, my sons, and many of our church members on our own personal journeys. I implore you to journey with us, your personal testimony starts today. See you on the path,

Cassandra Loggins

9

Preface: As You Begin...

The Journey To Wholeness & Holiness is conveniently presented for your daily reading and prayerful meditation and dietary discipline so that you may experience wholeness and holiness in Christ Jesus. This is not just another devotional book. In fact, it is unlike any other personal devotional book you have ever read. In *The Journey To Wholeness & Holiness*, you will learn what it means to encounter God, be thirsty for truth and eager for developing inner peace with God, and experience strength while on the journey.

In *The Journey To Wholeness & Holiness*, you will see the Spirit of the living God at work in your life like you have never witnessed. Along the way, you will be led by the Holy Spirit of God daily to learn the value of The Word of God and how God's Word helps you achieve wholeness and holiness.

If you have never read a personal, devotional book before, be prepared for a wonderful treat. You will never be the same. Your life change will be evident in just a few days while you step on the path of the journey. And for this reason, I would like to let you know how to read *The Journey To Wholeness & Holiness* for all it's worth.

The Journey To Wholeness & Holiness begins with a very practical introduction. Take your time and read the introduction prayerfully and faithfully. You don't want to miss any of your blessings. Following the introduction, the next major section in *The Journey To Wholeness & Holiness* is 40 days of fasting and prayer. This is the heart and soul of the journey. This section is designed for you to take your time and allow the Spirit of God to do deep work in your soul. Please take your time. Allow the Lord time to speak to your heart. You will be able to complete each exercise in 30 minutes or less. However, if you sense God telling to you to press on, then press on. Take your time. Enjoy each and every day.

The 40 days of fasting and prayer is about applying two very simple, yet powerful spiritual disciplines. The first discipline is that of prayer. Prayer is simply talking or engaging in a conversation with God. The second discipline is that of fasting. Fasting is a spiritual discipline of abstaining from eating food with a divine purpose or intent present in the heart of one engaged in fasting.

To help you achieve all God has in store for you let me give you the 5 easy steps for every traveler on the journey to wholeness and holiness. Step: 1) You are to read and meditate on the Scripture passage. Step: 2) You are to read the devotional message. Step: 3) You are to read the devotional prayer. Step: 4) You are to write your own prayer using A.C.T.S. [Adoration, Confession, Thanksgiving and Supplication (refer to Day 38)]. And Step: 5) You are to journal daily for 40 days.

The Journey To Wholeness & Holiness is work. Fasting and praying are some of the most difficult tasks Christians engage in on a daily basis. However, there are great benefits and blessings accompanied in the spiritual discipline of having a personal devotional life with God.

The next section in *The Journey To Wholeness & Holiness* is the conclusion. I call this section "Peaks and Valleys." Why? In this section, I am encouraging you to share the peaks (they are the profound joys) you experienced while on the journey. On the other hand, I am encouraging you to share about your valleys. Peaks and valleys are normal human realities. Learn the value of maximizing your peaks and managing your valleys. In the peaks and valleys section, you will notice that both are illustrated employing the same graphic depiction. I chose to do this purposefully. Often in the life of the Christian traveler, peaks and valleys are very similar. They are essence life's highs and lows.

11

What I want you to learn as a you travel the Christian journey is to maintain balance despite the depth of the pit or the high of the mountain top experience. It is my prayer that you will learn how to embrace both peaks and valleys. God uses peaks and valleys to teach us, to grow us and to mature us as His people.

Following the section on peaks and valleys, you will then be encouraged in "Continuing **The** Journey **(CTJ)**." Continuing the journey is just what it says, continuing the journey. We must realize that the journey is never complete until we see Jesus. So, my dear sister or brother, continue the journey. Don't stop your journey once the 40 days of prayer and fasting concludes. You've only just begun. Therefore to help you continue the journey, I have provided some helpful scripture passages for you.

The following section is rightly called "Tools for the Journey." Each tool is directly from the Word of God. These are excellent tools. You can trust every last word in The Journey's tool box. Remember, you are on a journey. You are not running the 100 meters. This book is not a sprint; *The Journey To Wholeness & Holiness* is a long distance run. Run to win Saints. But most of all, stay on the journey. Don't start and stop. Ask God to give you whatever it takes for you to cross the finish line a winner.

The last section of *The Journey To Wholeness & Holiness* provides a personal touch. You can read about the author. You can read about the author's place of ministerial service to both God and man. Finally, *The Journey To Wholeness & Holiness* closes with my future writings; writings that will help you enjoy your Christian journey. Remember, stay with it. You will be able to do what I learned to do when I was in the sixth grade.

I was chosen by my sixth grade performing arts teacher to be in our annual musical production. She came to me and said, "Robert you have been chosen to be in the annual sixth grade musical this year." I was shocked. Fear gripped me and I froze stiff like a dead man. I experienced a mental block in learning my seventeen lines in the musical as one of the key performers. However, when I listened to the words of our theme song, my fear evaporated into the thin air and I performed in the musical with ease. The song was from *The Sound of Music*, "Climb Every Mountain."[1]

Climb Ev'ry Mountain,
Ford Evr'y stream,
Follow Evr'y rainbow,
'Till you find your dream.

A dream that will need
All the love you can give,
Ev'ry day of your life
For as long as you live.

Climb ev'ry mountain,
Ford ev'ry stream,
Follow every rainbow,
Till you find your dream

A dream that will need
All the love you can give,
Ev'ry day of your life,
For as long as you live.

Climb ev'ry mountain,
Ford ev'ry stream,
Follow evr'y rainbow,
Till You Find Your Dream

---

[1] *The Sound of Music*, "Climb Every Mountain," http://www.lyrics007.com/Sound%20Of%20Music%20Lyrics/Climb%20 Every%20Mountain%20Lyrics.html.

The Journey To Wholeness & Holiness

Allow the lyrics of this song to enable you to relentlessly complete *The Journey To Wholeness & Holiness.* As you begin, you are one step closer toward achieving your goal.

Pastor   Robert   F.   Loggins

The Journey To Wholeness & Holiness

THE JOURNEY TO

wholeness
& HOLINESS

FASTING AND PRAYING

Introduction

I am so excited that you decided to pick up this life-changing book to begin your journey to wholeness and holiness. For many years, my congregation has been encouraging me to write a devotional book for the general public, and I am thrilled by their loving encouragement and gracious support. Here it is. The book is in your hands. Isn't the Lord, our God, a wonderful provider? That is why I want you to know that every word in this book has been prayed over, not only by the author, but also by every member of The WORD Is Alive Ministries. This is a work of God, and it is my desire that the Holy Spirit will truly set you free from the bondage of life's struggles and hindrances.

The focal passage, John 5:1-15, is the story of a man in need of a healing. The Bible does not give us the man's, name as he represents all of humanity. Jesus inquired of the crippled man, "Wilt thou be made whole?"

After this there was a feast of the Jews; and Jesus went up to Jerusalem. Now there is at Jerusalem by the sheep market a pool, which is called in the Hebrew tongue Bethesda, having five porches. In these lay a great multitude of impotent folk, of blind, halt, withered, waiting for the moving of the water. For an angel went down at a certain season into the pool, and troubled the water: whosoever then first after the troubling of the water stepped in was made whole of whatsoever disease he had. And a certain man was there, which had an infirmity thirty and eight years. When Jesus saw him lie, and knew that he had been now a long time in that case, he saith unto him, Wilt thou be made whole? The impotent man answered him, Sir, I have no man, when the water is troubled, to put me into the pool: but while I am

17

*coming, another steppeth down before me. Jesus saith
unto him, Rise, take up thy bed, and walk. And
immediately the man was made whole, and took up his
bed, and walked: and on the same day was the
sabbath. The Jews therefore said unto him that was
cured, It is the sabbath day: it is not lawful for thee to
carry thy bed. He answered them, He that made me
whole, the same said unto me, Take up thy bed, and
walk. Then asked they him, What man is that which
said unto thee, Take up thy bed, and walk? And he
that was healed wist not who it was: for Jesus had
conveyed himself away, a multitude being in that
place. Afterward Jesus findeth him in the temple, and
said unto him, Behold, thou art made whole: sin no
more, lest a worse thing come unto thee. The man
departed, and told the Jews that it was Jesus, which
had made him whole. And therefore did the Jews
persecute Jesus, and sought to slay him, because he
had done these things on the sabbath day.*

I do not know how long you have been crippled in
your spiritual walk with God, nor am I sure of your current
relationship with the Lord of the Sabbath; nonetheless, in
spite of your present standing with Christ, the Lord of the
Sabbath, He wants you to take it to the next level. God desires
a change in your life. He does not want you to continue
living a life devoid of devoted conviction and spiritual
growth. In order to do so, you must stop hanging around
people who seek to hold you hostage to your painful past,
thus, hindering you from a peace with God, which passes all
understanding.

It is time for you to embrace the heart of the Lord of
the Sabbath and be made whole. Step out of your crippled
condition and stop hanging around other folks who are

holding you down from being completely healed. God wants you to take up your bed and walk.

The Journey To Wholeness & Holiness will help you achieve the next step. Remember, it is only a step with the aid of the Lord of the Sabbath. The Lord of the Sabbath is with you. We possess a life-changing power endowed to us by a loving God, and prayer and fasting is a part of our constituted means to achieve wholeness and holiness.

Now let the journey begin!

Pastor Robert F. Loggins

ADVENTURERS

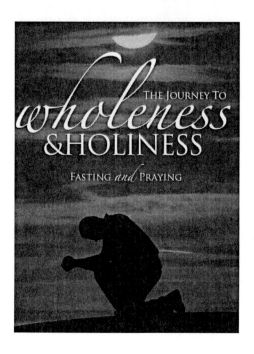

"All great adventures begins and ends at,
the throne of grace."

— a wise saying taken from the heart and soul of Hebrews 4:16.

Dear Adventurers:

Wholeness is what we want at The WORD Is Alive Ministries (TWIAM). This is what was on the heart of our Lord and Savior Jesus Christ, when He asked the lame man at the pool, "Wilt thou be made whole?"[2] This year marks the continuation of our church's "Spiritual Journey" in which we are plunging into the spiritual depth of the loving arms of the Lord of Sabbath to witness the power and presence of God in our church, by living for God's glory in a new and fresh way. My sincere prayer as pastor-teacher of The WORD Is Alive Ministries is that the Lord Jesus Christ will show us the way He wants us to go. Furthermore, our prayer is that through the power and movement of the Holy Spirit, God will help us appreciate and enjoy a closer walk with Him. Our prayer is that we will all be able to shout with great joy.

Hear Our Prayer O Lord!
Make Us Whole

Dear Lord, we are your people.
We want to be made whole.
So, lead us.
Make us anew.
Fill us with your Spirit.
Heal us.
Prepare us to meet you each day on your terms.
Dear Lord, there is no one like you.
Dear Lord, there is no one like you.
So, yes, LORD!
We want to be made completely whole.
Amen and Praise God!

---

[2] John 5:6, KJV.

What Is Your Focus?

Our focus in this adventure is to grasp the heart and soul of the action that Jesus took to make a lame man whole. As God's people, we need wholeness. We, the members of The WORD Is Alive Ministries, a disciple-making church, are now embarking on the journey. When we step out on faith, in the Lord of the Sabbath, as we journey to wholeness and holiness, John 5:1 – 15, joy will burst forth from our inner being. The journey is a journey of joy. Let us enjoy the journey. We are indeed the people of God, and we are entering into wholeness and holiness right now. Our objective is simple, "Let us take up our bed and walk," (John 5:8). So, are you ready? Are you ready to begin the journey to wholeness and holiness with God?

Change Me, O Lord! Change Me, I PRAY!

This devotional book seeks to enhance your time with God each morning and throughout the entire day. Please consider the following.

Changed Habits & New Disciplines

You are changing habits. Like any new discipline, this will take effort. Do not be discouraged if you do not experience immediate gratification. Continue to be faithful to the journey and the rewards will come.

22

Finding A Quiet Place

It helps to go to bed early for the best early morning time. Find a quiet place for your meeting with God.

The War Of The Flesh

Understand that Satan and your flesh will war against you in the days ahead. Satan will try to distract you; at times you may think that things are getting worse. But you will soon come to find out that God is on our side and you are "More than a conqueror" (Romans 8:37).

Remaining Committed To The WORD

Let others help you. Stay in regular contact with others who are in contact with God. Stay in the WORD every day. Do not miss inspirational times, encouragement times, worship times, fellowship times and discipleship small group times. God wants to nurture you, and He wants to love you with Tender Loving Care (TLC). This is agapē (i.e., the love of God, John 3:16-17). Keep a Spiritual Journal, and be determined to cross the finish line and pay the price. Let the Lord lead you. Keep the faith. You can make it. God is on your side. You are in Christ (2 Corinthians 5:17). In the days ahead, you will see a difference in your life. God will change you. He will change your habits. He will change your heart. He will give you the mind of Christ as wholeness in Christ emerges from the inner being of your soul to the outer dress of your spirit-anointed radiance.

There Is Freedom In His Presence

Use this devotional book as a guide for your journey. Let the Lord lead you into His wonderful and magnificent presence. Do not let the devotional book bind you. Allow the Holy Spirit to remain in charge throughout the entire journey. God knows what He is doing with you as you travel. Remember that He is God! He is the God and Guide of the journey. Remember, your ultimate goal is to glorify God and develop intimacy with the person of the Lord Jesus Christ.

Be Holy!

The Bible teaches us to be holy as opposed to engaging in holy things or holy activities. Holiness is more than activity; it is a matter of the wholeness of one's heart. When our hearts are bent toward God's heavenly throne, we will be holy. The Apostle Paul was right when he reminded us with these insightful words of encouragement and admonition to be holy. Holiness does not imply being absolute in human perfection. Holiness suggests to us the position of being set apart for service unto both God and man. Holiness is God's way of separating us from the world. We are in the world, yet we are not of the world. We are the righteousness of God, made anew daily by God's amazing grace and loving-kindness. We belong to God and were purchased by the blood of Jesus at the cross on Golgotha's hill. Whole and holy, that's who we are. Today, let us exalt Him as the Lord of the Sabbath.

God Exalted Living!

Wherefore God also hath highly exalted him, and given him a name which is above every name: That at the name of Jesus every knee should bow, of things in heaven, and things in earth, and things under the earth. And that every tongue should confess that Jesus Christ is Lord, to the glory of God the Father.[3]

Let us exalt Christ! Be holy! Journey now!

---

[3] Philippians 2:9-11, "The Exaltation of the Christ of God."

DAY 1

PRAYER
AND FASTING

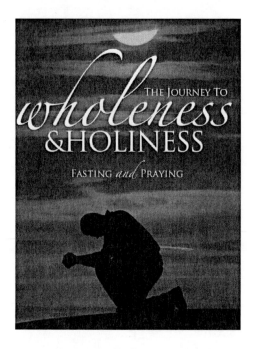

"Prayer is the natural outgushing of a soul in communion with Jesus."

– Spurgeon (Editor, Robert Hall), *The Power of Prayer in a Believer's Life, p.30.*

Day 1
Prayer And Fasting: Tool For A Successful Journey
The Model Prayer
When We Pray

Most Christians refer to Matthew 6:9 – 15 as "The Lord's Prayer," however, The Lord's Prayer is found in the Gospel of John, chapter 17. This was the prayer that Jesus prayed, as He prepared to go to Calvary to die for the sins of the world. But, the question remains. What was the purpose of the prayer model recorded in Matthew 6:9 – 15? I believe the purpose was to teach us how to pray. That is why Matthew 6:9-15 is referred to as "The Model Prayer," whereas, John chapter 17 is identified as The Lord's Prayer. So, as we journey to wholeness and holiness employing The Model Prayer, God's power will be given to us from on high like we have never witnessed in our lives in times past. We will be able to achieve success at the next level in our journey with God, not because we are perfect people, but because we now know how to pray with power and purpose. That is why James the Elder declares in agreement with Christ, the Son of God; "Prayer is powerful and effective."[4] Listen now to the teaching Christ provides in The Model Prayer.

Read & Meditate Matthew 6:6 – 15 (HCSB)

But when you pray, go into your private room, shut your door, and pray to your Father who is in secret. And your

---

[4] James 5:16b, says, "The effectual fervent prayer of a righteous man availeth much." The word "availeth" suggests to the travelers that this type of prayer gets the job done.

Father who sees in secret will reward you. When you pray, don't babble like the idolaters, since they imagine they'll be heard for their many words. Don't be like them, because your Father knows the things you need before you ask Him. Therefore, you should pray like this: Our Father in heaven, Your name be honored as holy. Your kingdom come. Your will be done on earth as it is in heaven. Give us today our daily bread. And forgive us our debts, as we also have forgiven our debtors. And do not bring us into temptation, but deliver us from the evil one. [For Yours is the kingdom and the power and the glory forever. Amen.] For if you forgive people their wrongdoing, your heavenly Father will forgive you as well. But if you don't forgive people, your Father will not forgive your wrongdoing.

ONE WAY TO PRAY

This is how the Lord Jesus Christ instructed His Disciples to pray while on the journey. He did not tell them that this was the only way to pray. Rather, He told them that this was an effective example of one prayer model.

"Our Father in heaven..."

This has to do with our God. It is a matter of His place of position. He sits in heaven to watch over us. He cares for us. He understands us, and He is always there for us in times of need throughout the journey.

"...Hallowed be your name..."

This has to do with the holiness of God. God is holy. His name is holy, and when we pray we are to respect and reverence His wonderful, mighty and glorious name. To not respect His name cripples us on the journey.

"...Your kingdom come..."

This suggests to us God's dynamic dominion. God is at work building His kingdom in each of us. Moreover, as we pray, we long for the coming of God's kingdom. The journey is long and often difficult, but our eyes are on the kingdom. We know that His kingdom will come. That is because, wherever the kingdom of God is, there is always a place of peace and rest. Richard J. Foster in his magnificent work, *Prayer: Finding The Heart's True Home*, writes concerning the prayer of rest.

> Through the Prayer of Rest God places his children in the eye of the storm. When all around us is chaos and confusion, deep within we know stability and serenity. In the midst of intense personal struggle we are still and relaxed. While a thousand frustrations seek to distract us, we remain focused and attentive. This is the fruit of the Prayer of Rest.[5]

When we pray for the coming of His kingdom, we are praying for all of that which God is and ever would be to rest upon us all as His chosen people. The blessing is ours. God's kingdom will come. Therefore, remain focused on the journey to wholeness and holiness.

---

[5] Richard J. Foster, *Prayer: Finding The Heart's True Home* (New York: HarperCollins Publishers, 1992), p.93.

29

"...Your will be done on earth as it is in heaven."

The journey to wholeness and holiness is all about doing God's will. The will of God is an expression of the heart of God's deepest desire for us as His people. The will of God denotes two key concepts of His eternal nature. First, there is the "Perfect Will of God." Second, there is the "Permissive Will of God". The Perfect Will of God has to do with what God dearly wants for all of His creation. God wants us to be at rest and peace in His Perfect Will. However, the Permissive Will of God is an expression of man's freewill. God gives us freewill in our humanity to embrace or not to embrace His Perfect Will. In short, God gives us a choice. God does not force us to do what He wants us to do. He simply provides for us the opportunity to do what is within our own freewill. In Genesis 3, Adam and Eve chose not God's best. They chose sin. Their willful act of disobedience led to their expulsion from the Garden of Eden, but how do we avoid "Edenmistic"[6] expulsion? Simple, submit daily to the will of God.

"Give us today our daily bread."

Our food for the journey is our *"daily bread."* It is the manna of God, which is the living bread of eternal life in Jesus Christ our Lord. This bread has to do with daily feeding on God's Holy Word. What we want to do is to feed on God's Word, while we travel on our journey. During our

---

[6] "Edenmistic" is a word expression denoting the character of Adam and Eve following the fall in Genesis 3. Genesis 3:1, says, "Now the serpent..." (NIV). Sin entered the Garden of Eden, and man fell into sinful disobedience and God expelled mankind from paradise. Romans 5:12 says, "Therefore, just as sin entered the world through one man, and death through sin, and in this way death came to all men, because all sinned" (NIV).

time of fasting and prayer, we want the Word of God to feed us until we want no more. We want Him to fill us. We want Him to fill us full of more of God and less of us so that we might know Him more and serve Him better.

"Forgive us our debts, as we also have forgiven our debtors."

A debt is an infraction or a sin against either God or man. Sin strains our relationship with God, and our journey becomes more difficult. As Christians, we do not lose our salvation; we simply lose the closeness of our fellowship with Almighty God and our journey is more stressful. This is not good for our Christian witness and spiritual and physical health. That is why Jesus admonishes us to forgive each other. As we learn to forgive each other of the wrong done to us, we are saying to God this: "Dear Lord, since I have forgiven my brother or my sister, please Lord, forgive me, as I have forgiven my fellowman or woman." As we focus on staying on the journey to wholeness and holiness, let us learn the power of forgiveness. Let us do for others what our Lord and Savior Jesus Christ did for us at Calvary. He died! He literally, died to self. Death to self, promotes the success of the journey.

"And lead us not into temptation, but deliver us from the evil one."

Deliverance is what we need, deliverance from self into the Savior. The journey to wholeness and holiness makes deliverance a reality. However, if we repeatedly fall to all types of temptations, then God delays our deliverance from bondage. Delayed deliverance is a satanic invitation off the path of wholeness and holiness. We want immediate deliverance. Immediate deliverance is deliverance from the

31

power of the evil one. The evil one is none other than Satan, Lucifer, and the Devil who is none other than The Prince of Darkness and Deception (Ephesians 6).

"For if you forgive men when they sin against you, your heavenly Father will also forgive you."

If you want to have a successful journey to wholeness and holiness, employ the personal choice of forgiveness. It works, and you will find complete peace. We all need peace – peace with God. That is the kind of peace you and I will find as precious jewels in the midst of the journey. The journey to wholeness and holiness is all of God and none of man. Man is a sinner in need of forgiveness. Once forgiven by God, man now knows how to do for others what Jesus did for him. Forgive! When you exercise the power of forgiveness, your journey will be a joy and not a job. Do not wait to be forgiven. You forgive even when you don't think that you have been forgiven.

"But if you do not forgive men their sins, your Father will not forgive your sins."

If you do not forgive then do not expect God to forgive you. When you refuse to be a forgiver, your journey will be hard. The road to success is not paved with peace. Forgive and then watch God do a new thing in and through you each day. The journey to wholeness and holiness is where the power is, the peace is and the Person of Jesus Christ is. There is no other way than being with God!

THE WONDERFUL NATURE OF THE JOURNEY

What a wonderful place to begin your journey with God! Tomorrow you will begin your *Spiritual Journey To Wholeness & Holiness* with God. Prepare to get a good night's sleep for your first morning of coming into the presence of your heavenly Father. He is waiting for you. He is looking with great anticipation to meet you early Monday morning. Spend some quality time in prayer the night before. You may want to spend time in prayer with your immediate family as well. You may want to educate your children as to why fasting and praying is important to you, as a follower of the Lord Jesus Christ, as you journey to wholeness and holiness. Then allow your children or family members or friends to ask you questions. Do not worry if you cannot answer all of their questions. Take it to God in prayer. This is going to be such a wonderful spiritual journey to wholeness and holiness. God is waiting on you. He wants you to know beyond any doubt that you can "be made whole" (John 5). In fact, a life in which one can live is a whole life. This life is complete in God. This is how you are going to begin this wonderful, spiritual journey to wholeness and holiness with God.

REFRESHED & READY TO MEET GOD

Ask God to awaken you refreshed and ready to meet with Him. Pray for at least seven other people in The WORD Is Alive Ministries each week of your journey. Call them up and offer words of encouragement. Seeking God on your knees leads to keeping the unity of the spirit through the bonds of peace (Ephesians 4).

Know The Enemy!

Ask God to bind the Enemy from distracting you from your special time with your Heavenly Father.

Anticipate The Rewards!

Go to bed anticipating the rewards of this time together with the LORD God.

Thank God Now!

Thank God in advance for what He is going to do in your life.

Engage In Daily Acts Of Kindness!

Begin to consider seven premeditated acts of kindness that you will do every week. This is one a day.

Trust God Whole-Heartedly!

Ask God if He would have you "Trust Him with All Your Heart." Ask Him to give you opportunities to share your Faith with others.

Rise & Shine!

Set your alarm to arise early tomorrow! God is waiting on you. Praise His Name!

FASTING APPROACH: FOOD GUIDELINES

1. No beef.
2. No pork.
3. No lamb.
4. The fast allows for eating of fish and fowls.
5. The fast allows for eating of wheat and other natural grain bread products.
6. No fried fish or fowls, vegetables and bread products.
7. No candy or desserts, however, gum and breath-mints are permitted.
8. The fast allows for eating fruit (fresh/canned in natural juices or lite/frozen and the like).
9. The fast allows for drinking all types of juices (Kool-Aid without sugar).
10. Cold or hot tea and coffee are permitted. However, such beverages must be prepared without processed sugar. Equal and related sweeteners are permitted.

Note: As with any significant dietary change, please consult your physician or healthcare professional, especially if you have diabetes, are pregnant or nursing.

THE JOURNEY TO WHOLENESS & HOLINESS

Jesus Christ is God's only begotten Son.[7] He is the Second Person of the Godhead.[8] We need to remember, Jesus is always present, as we daily seek God's heart. Therefore, look for God's activity around you, as you daily travel on your journey, by doing what Christ commands, "Seek and ye shall find, knock and the door shall be open."[9] Clearly state in second person a record of your journey to wholeness and holiness. The Second Person of the Godhead is the Lord Jesus Christ. We need to remember, He is always present as we seek God's heart. Look for God's activity around you on your daily journey. "Seek and ye shall find, knock and the door shall be open."[10] Now at this point, there is an expression, which comes to mind from my childhood saying, "Trust in the Lord with all your heart my son and never depend on human knowledge, intellectual understanding or earthly insight but only on the God in three persons: Father, Son and Holy Spirit."[11] Such trust elevates one's joy, peace, patience, love[12] and humility by causing the human soul to be at rest completely in God's sovereign presence and awesome power.

---

[7] John 3:16, "Jesus Christ, God's Son."

[8] The Godhead is a term denoting God in three persons: God the Father, God the Son and God the Holy Spirit. See, Matthew 3:13-17. "Jesus" is the Son. "A voice from heaven" is the Father. And finally, "the Spirit of God descending like a dove" is the Holy Spirit.

[9] Matthew 7:7, "Seek God," (paraphrased).

[10] Matthew 7:7, "Seek God," (paraphrased).

[11] This is a saying from my childhood.

[12] Galatians 5:22-23, "The Fruit of the Spirit," refers to ones character. God develops human character, as we remain faithful in continuing to travel on the journey to wholeness and holiness.

Being Personal With God!

Furthermore, it is also my pastoral prayer that the Lord Jesus Christ will help every one of us to understand that it is possible to travel the journey to wholeness and holiness successfully. God is the source of our strength. God will not let us down. God is there to help us. He is always there in the person of the Holy Spirit of God. God gave us His Son and the Son sent us God's Spirit – The Holy Spirit to make sure that we will have a successful journey.

Being Made Whole!

That is why Jesus said to the lame man at the pool of Bethesda, "Do you want to be made whole?"[13] As we travel on the journey, God's Holy Spirit challenges us to wholeness and wholeness is what we need. God bless you and keep you in His eternal care and may His Love give you all that you need to successfully complete your journey. Remember, Love Is The Most Excellent Way! "Do you want to be made whole"?[14] If so, then repeat these words, "Yes, Lord, make me whole," and He will.

---

[13] John 5, NIV.
[14] Ibid.

DAY 2

YOU ARE NOT ALONE

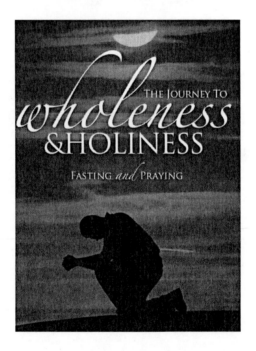

"He who has a *why* to live can bear with almost any *how*."

– Nietzsche, from Vicktor E. Frankl,
Man's Search for Meaning, p. 9.

Day 2

Thought for Today: You Are Not Alone!

Read and Meditate: 1 Kings 18:16 – 24 (KJV)

So Obadiah went to meet Ahab, and told him: and Ahab went to meet Elijah. And it came to pass, when Ahab saw Elijah, that Ahab said unto him, Art thou he that troubleth Israel? And he answered, I have not troubled Israel; but thou, and thy father's house, in that ye have forsaken the commandments of the LORD, and thou hast followed Baalim. Now therefore send, and gather to me all Israel unto mount Carmel, and the prophets of Baal four hundred and fifty, and the prophets of the groves four hundred, which eat at Jezebel's table. So Ahab sent unto all the children of Israel, and gathered the prophets together unto mount Carmel. And Elijah came unto all the people, and said, How long halt ye between two opinions? if the LORD be God, follow him: but if Baal, then follow him. And the people answered him not a word. Then said Elijah unto the people, I, even I only, remain a prophet of the LORD; but Baal's prophets are four hundred and fifty men. Let them therefore give us two bullocks; and let them choose one bullock for themselves, and cut it in pieces, and lay it on wood, and put no fire under: and I will dress the other bullock, and lay it on wood, and put no fire under: And call ye on the name of your gods, and I will call on the name of the LORD: and the God that answereth by fire, let him be God. And all the people answered and said, It is well spoken.

The prophet Elijah had to learn like many of us today that we are not in this all by ourselves. Although we cannot see God, He is still there. God is always present. The prophet Elijah had to learn this life lesson from personal experience. He had to come to a place in his life, where all he had was God.. There are times when as a faithful follower of Jesus Christ, all you will have is God, so remember, you are not alone! I submit that this is the time when God is supernaturally present. When God comes near you; will know it. When you come near to God, He will know you and you will know Him even more.

Prayer: Dear Lord, please come near. Lord, I need your touch. I need your love. I need you more each day, dear Lord. Jesus, my life has been wasted in the wasteland of human failures, and I have come to the end of my steps. I have stumbled and fallen in the pit of shame and despair, and only you and you only dear Lord, are qualified to lift me from the pit to the palace. Here I am. I am yours. I am all yours. Please, come help me today. I am not alone in Jesus' name, Amen!

Personalize Prayer: Write your own prayer, using A.C.T.S. Refer to The Journey's Preface for help.

_____

_____

_____

_____

_____

_____

_____

_____

_____

Prayer Journal Notes: What do you do when you are feeling alone? Then determine what God wants you to do when you feel that you are all alone. Develop a spiritual plan to address your loneliness, and then make a commitment to your Heavenly Father that you will overcome the spirit of loneliness with "longingness"[15] for God.

_____

_____

_____

_____

_____

_____

_____

_____

_____

Pray for men.
Fast 'til 12'clock midnight.

_____

[15] "Longingness" is what I call a deep expression of desire and thirst to know the heart of God experientially.

42

The Journey To Wholeness & Holiness

DAY 3

I SEEK THEE

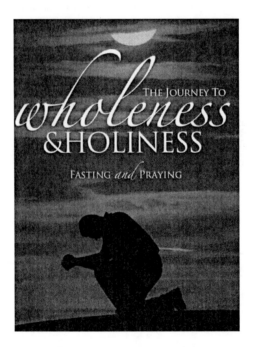

"The pouring out of His soul is the divine
meaning of intercession,"

– Andrew Murray & C. H. Spurgeon, *The Believer's Secret of
Intercession,*(Complier, L. G. Parkhurst, Jr., p. 45.

Day 3

I Seek Thee In The Morning

Read and Meditate: Psalm 5:3 – 12 (KJV)

My voice shalt thou hear in the morning, O LORD; in the morning will I direct my prayer unto thee, and will look up. For thou art not a God that hath pleasure in wickedness: neither shall evil dwell with thee. The foolish shall not stand in thy sight: thou hatest all workers of iniquity. Thou shalt destroy them that speak leasing: the LORD will abhor the bloody and deceitful man. But as for me, I will come into thy house in the multitude of thy mercy: and in thy fear will I worship toward thy holy temple. Lead me, O LORD, in thy righteousness because of mine enemies; make thy way straight before my face. For there is no faithfulness in their mouth; their inward part is very wickedness; their throat is an open sepulchre; they flatter with their tongue. Destroy thou them, O God; let them fall by their own counsels; cast them out in the multitude of their transgressions; for they have rebelled against thee. But let all those that put their trust in thee rejoice: let them ever shout for joy, because thou defendest them: let them also that love thy name be joyful in thee. For thou, LORD, wilt bless the righteous; with favour wilt thou compass him as with a shield.

The heart of the faithful one who walks with the Lord on the journey is a heart of hunger for God. To hunger for God is to seek not only His face, but to seek to know His perfect will. The will of God is not something that God hides from us as disciples of the Lord Jesus Christ. God wants us to know Him. God is not trying to be difficult. He is the God

45

of Divine Invitation. He is saying to us, "I love you and I want you to know all of me. I am open to your investigation. So come. I am waiting on you. Come and learn. I want to see you soon." Oh, my dear brother and my dear sister, seek thee Him in the morning.

Prayer: Lord where are you? I do not know where you are. Then, I hear a still small voice speak to my inner most part. "I have not moved. Do you know where you are?" Lord, I thank you that I desire to seek you daily, early in the morning: when the sun is fresh; when the dewdrops are glistening on the tender needles of uncut blades of still quiet green grass, my heart says, "Lord, I seek Thou face." Lord, you are always there. I love You, Lord. Thank You loving me just the way I am!

Personalize Prayer: Write your own prayer, using A.C.T.S. Refer to The Journey's Preface for help.

_____

_____

_____

_____

_____

_____

_____

_____

_____

Prayer Journal Notes: Make it your objective to "seek God in the morning." Do it now! Do not wait! Will you do it for yourself? Will you do it for God's glory? Please answer: Yes, or no!

_____

_____

_____

_____

_____

_____

_____

_____

_____

Pray one hour for mothers and babies.
Fast all day.

The Journey To Wholeness & Holiness

DAY 4

IN THE PIT

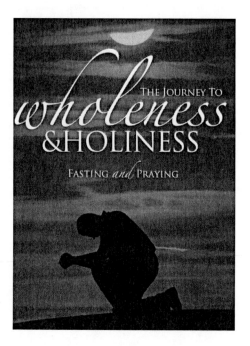

"Weak stomachs prefer bland diets,
but strong stomachs never refuse any meat
set before them; all fare is alike to them."

– William Gurnall, *The Christian in Complete Armour*, p. 394.

Day 4

Life In The Pit

Read and Meditate: Psalm 88:1 – 18 (KJV)

O lord God of my salvation, I have cried day and night before thee: Let my prayer come before thee: incline thine ear unto my cry; For my soul is full of troubles: and my life draweth nigh unto the grave. I am counted with them that go down into the pit: I am as a man that hath no strength: Free among the dead, like the slain that lie in the grave, whom thou rememberest no more: and they are cut off from thy hand. Thou hast laid me in the lowest pit, in darkness, in the deeps. Thy wrath lieth hard upon me, and thou hast afflicted me with all thy waves. Selah. Thou hast put away mine acquaintance far from me; thou hast made me an abomination unto them: I am shut up, and I cannot come forth. Mine eye mourneth by reason of affliction: LORD, I have called daily upon thee, I have stretched out my hands unto thee. Wilt thou shew wonders to the dead? Shall the dead arise and praise thee? Selah. Shall thy lovingkindness be declared in the grave? Or thy faithfulness in destruction? Shall thy wonders be known in the dark? And thy righteousness in the land of forgetfulness? But unto thee have I cried, O LORD; and in the morning shall my prayer prevent thee. LORD, why castest thou off my soul? Why hidest thou thy face from me? I am afflicted and ready to die from my youth up: while I suffer thy terrors I am distracted. Thy fierce wrath goeth over me; thy terrors have cut me off. They came round about me daily like water; they compassed me about together. Lover and friend hast thou put far from me, and mine acquaintance into darkness.

The Christian life is not always on top of the mountain. Sometimes it is a life "in the pit." Life in the pit is the pits! No one wants to live life in the pit. However, there are many lessons that one can learn from experiencing life in the pit.

I believe that for many of us who seek God to the next level in our Christian endeavor, God invites us to a "pit party." In fact, a pit party helps us celebrate deeper spiritual growth and Christian maturity. Neither you nor I will ever become what God desires us to be, without attending our own personal sacred pit party.

If you are in a pit, celebrate! God is deepening you. He is deepening your faith. He is expanding your future. He is fueling your fire. Get excited and praise God! You have finally made it. You have made it to your own personal celebration, your pit party. You will grow as if you have never grown before.

Moreover, those who attempt to bypass the pit will never handle the great successes of the mountaintop. Remember this. The deeper the pit, the more powerful and profound the praise! Learn how to celebrate your personal pit parties. It will not be like this always. God is only developing you for His greater glory.

Prayer: Father, thank you for blessing me with my pit. I am so thankful that you thought enough of me to throw a party like this just for little old me. I know that you must really love me to allow me to go through all this wonderful pain. That is the pain of the pit. Dear Jesus, people may see me in my pit, but they just don't know what you are doing down in the pit with me. Hallelujah! Hallelujah! Praise the Lord!

Personalize Prayer: Write your own prayer, using A.C.T.S. Refer to The Journey's Preface for help.

_____

_____

_____

_____

_____

_____

_____

_____

Prayer Journal Notes: What pit are you in now? Or have you even been in a pit? Tell how God lifted you out of your pit. Or tell God thank you for the pit that you are in today.

_____

_____

_____

_____

_____

_____

_____

_____

_____

Pray three times: morning, noon and night.
Fast for one meal.

The Journey To Wholeness & Holiness

DAY 5

HIS THRONE

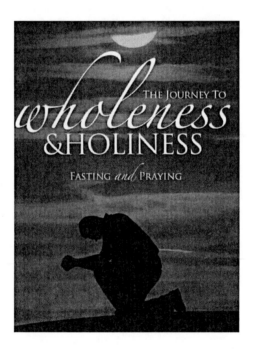

"The Cross is the pathway to life in Christ."

– Andrew Murray, *The Secret of Spiritual Strength*, p. 69.

Day 5

The Journey To His Throne

Read and Meditate Hebrews 4:14 – 16 (HCSB)

Therefore since we have a great high priest who has passed through the heavens—Jesus the Son of God—let us hold fast to the confession. For we do not have a high priest who is unable to sympathize with our weaknesses, but One who has been tested in every way as we are, yet without sin. Therefore let us approach the throne of grace with boldness, so that we may receive mercy and find grace to help us at the proper time.

You can approach the throne of grace with confidence. Why is this so important to know? Because you are a Child of the Most High God and God knows you by name! Grace is what we need: G.R.A.C.E. is God's Riches At Christ's Expense! G.R.A.C.E. is a picture of the cross at Calvary. At Calvary, Jesus died. At Calvary, G.R.A.C.E. gave up the ghost. Thank God for what happened on Calvary's cross.

A – las! and did my Savior bleed? And did my Sov-'reign died? Would He devote that sacred head For such a worm as I? At the cross, at the cross where I first saw the light, And the burden of my heart rolled a-way – (rolled a-way) – It was there by faith I received my sight, And now I am happy all the day![16]

---

[16]T. B. Boyd, III, "At the Cross," *The New National Baptist Hymnal* (Nashville: National Baptist Publishing Board, 1977), 79.

Now, I am prepared to journey to the throne of God, without any of life's problems hindering me given the aid of Calvary's cross. Lord, focus is every man's need.

> The world behind me, the cross before me, The world behind me, the cross before me; The world behind me, the cross before me; No turning back, no turning back.[17]

---

[17] "I Have Decided To Follow Jesus," *Logos Library System Hymnal* [An Indian Prince, as sung in Garo, Assam; Folk melody from India; I Have Decided to Follow Jesus (Indian Triad?); Matt. 8:19-20; Luke 9:61-2; Matt. 16:24; Mark 8] (Oak Harbor: Logos Research Systems, Inc., 1997).

Prayer: Dear Lord I just want to say, "Thank you". You have made yourself so available to me. I can talk with you any time I want. You are never too busy to share your heart with me. However, I am the problem. I do not always want to be honest and open to you, My Lord. Dear Lord, help. Please, help in Jesus' Name, Amen!

Personalize Prayer: Write your own prayer, using A.C.T.S. Refer to The Journey's Preface for help.

_____

_____

_____

_____

_____

_____

_____

_____

_____

Prayer Journal Notes: Take this time to write about times you have approached the throne of God in prayer. What did you do to overcome your fear?

_____
_____
_____
_____
_____
_____
_____
_____
_____

Pray one hour on your knees for a habit you have.
Fast for one meal.

The Journey To Wholeness & Holiness

DAY 6

SODOM, GET OUT!

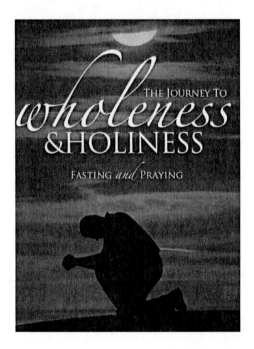

"Churches get in ruts only because individuals get in ruts.
It is impossible that the church should do
anything that individuals do not do."

– A. W. Tozer (Compiler, James L. Snyder),
Rut, Rot or Revival: The Condition of the Church, p.34.

Day 6

Pray For Sodom

Read and Meditate: Genesis 18:16 – 33 (KJV)

And the men rose up from thence, and looked toward Sodom: and Abraham went with them to bring them on the way And the LORD said, Shall I hide from Abraham that thing which I do; Seeing that Abraham shall surely become a great and mighty nation, and all the nations of the earth shall be blessed in him? For I know him, that he will command his children and his household after him, and they shall keep the way of the LORD, to do justice and judgment; that the LORD may bring upon Abraham that which he hath spoken of him. And the LORD said, Because the cry of Sodom and Gomorrah is great, and because their sin is very grievous; I will go down now, and see whether they have done altogether according to the cry of it, which is come unto me; and if not, I will know. And the men turned their faces from thence, and went toward Sodom: but Abraham stood yet before the LORD. And Abraham drew near, and said, Wilt thou also destroy the righteous with the wicked? Peradventure there be fifty righteous within the city: wilt thou also destroy and not spare the place for the fifty righteous that are therein? That be far from thee to do after this manner, to slay the righteous with the wicked: and that the righteous should be as the wicked, that be far from thee: Shall not the Judge of all the earth do right? And the LORD said, If I find in Sodom fifty righteous within the city, then I will spare all the place for their sakes. And Abraham answered and said, Behold now, I have taken upon me to speak unto the LORD, which am but dust and ashes:

Peradventure there shall lack five of the fifty righteous: wilt thou destroy all the city for lack of five? And he said, If I find there forty and five, I will not destroy it. And he spake unto him yet again, and said, Peradventure there shall be forty found there. And he said, I will not do it for forty's sake. And he said unto him, Oh let not the LORD be angry, and I will speak: Peradventure there shall thirty be found there. And he said, I will not do it, if I find thirty there. And he said, Behold now, I have taken upon me to speak unto the LORD: Peradventure there shall be twenty found there. And he said, I will not destroy it for twenty's sake. And he said, Oh let not the LORD be angry, and I will speak yet but this once: Peradventure ten shall be found there. And he said, I will not destroy it for ten's sake. And the LORD went his way, as soon as he had left communing with Abraham: and Abraham returned unto his place.

We need to pray for those who dwell in the city of Sodom. We need to pray that they will get out of the city of Sodom immediately. The city of Sodom is symbolic of man's sinfulness in the superlative degree. The Bible says that man is a sinner. Man is a sinner in need of a Savior. All men need salvation. All men need God to get them out of the city of Sodom, now! The city of Sodom, according to Old Testament literature, being a place of death and destruction, operates with an evil license to destroy its inhabitants. Spiritual forces of evil in heavenly places are often fueled by the scorching desert winds of narcissistic arrogance in the city of Sodom. Yet, because of the loving grace of God, God is concerned about every soul in the city of Sodom. God wants all men to be saved, even if they are Sodomites. That is why we need to pray to our heavenly Father to get us out of the city of Sodom. The Bible says, "The soul that sinneth, it shall die."[18] "For all have sinned, and come short of the glory of God."[19] "There is a way which seemeth right unto a man, but the end thereof are the ways of death."[20] God hates sin, but God loves the sinner. God wants to destroy sin, but God seeks to save sinners.

That is why we need to pray for those who are still residing in the city of Sodom today. Are you praying for anyone that you know, who maybe a resident of the city of Sodom? Are you pleading to your heavenly Father to get them out of the city of Sodom right now?

Every Christian today, needs to pray for those who will die in the city of Sodom, if the Lord does not get them out. We need to pray for the lost and dying souls living in the sin-sick city of Sodom. God is waiting on us to pray with power and conviction to win the battle for souls of the city of Sodom. Get out of Sodom! Get out now!

---

[18] Ezekiel 18:4b, "The sinful soul shall experience eternal death." This is known as separation from God. KJV.
[19] Romans 3:23, "All Sin!" KJV.
[20] Proverbs 14:12, "Sin leads to death." KJV.

Prayer: Dear Jesus I have come to realize that Sodom is closer than I thought. Sodom is where I live. Sodom is the sinfulness of my inner man. It is the place of my deepest personal struggles. It is a place of shame. It is where I live. No one can see my Sodom life, like my Heavenly Father, The Lord God Almighty. Jesus, I need Thee. Help me, I pray. Help me to get out of Sodom right now! Time is of the essence. Get out of Sodom now! Do it now! It is never too late to change. God is able to help you. Please let Him. He helps each of us in the Name of the Father, the Name of the Son and the Name of the Holy Spirit, Amen!

Personalize Prayer: Write your own prayer, using A.C.T.S. Refer to The Journey's Preface for help.

_____
_____
_____
_____
_____
_____
_____
_____
_____
_____

Prayer Journal Notes: The thing that every Christian has to understand is that each of us has our own personal Sodom. Paul calls it the "thorn in the flesh." Paul comes to understand just how weak he really was apart from his own personal efforts to live the life of the law. That is why Christians have to understand how God's wonderful grace works on their behalf. In 2 Corinthians 12:7 – 10, the Apostle Paul says,

> *...especially because of the extraordinary revelations. Therefore, so that I would not exalt myself, a thorn in the flesh was given to me, a messenger of Satan to torment me so I would not exalt myself. Concerning this, I pleaded with the Lord three times to take it away from me. But He said to me, "My grace is sufficient for you, for power is perfected in weakness." Therefore, I will most gladly boast all the more about my weaknesses, so that Christ's power may reside in me. So because of Christ, I am pleased in weaknesses, in insults, in catastrophes, in persecutions, and in pressures. For when I am weak, then I am strong. (HCSB)*

Tell how God has used your weakness or your Sodom to give you strength. Now remember I am not attempting to celebrate your Sodom or your weakness or your fallen sinful condition. I simply want you to know how to learn how to allow God's Holy Spirit to use you in spite of your limitations and then trust God to help you with your "thorn in the flesh, a messenger of Satan," to torment you and to keep you humble. Talk to God, now, as you take your journey to wholeness and holiness.

_____

_____

_____

_____

_____

_____
_____
_____
_____

Pray three times: morning, noon and night for all nations. Fast for one meal.

The Journey To Wholeness & Holiness

DAY 7

STRENGTHENED HANDS

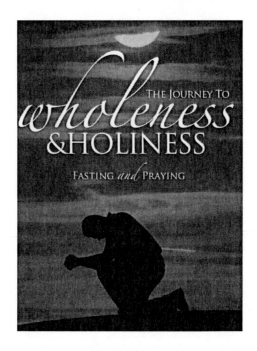

"I will greet this day with love in my heart."

– Og Mandino, *The Greatest Salesman in the World*, p. 58.

Day 7

The Kind of Prayer That Strengthens Hands

Read and Meditate   Nehemiah 6:5 – 9 (KJV)

Then sent Sanballat his servant unto me in like manner the fifth time with an open letter in his hand; Wherein was written, It is reported among the heathen, and Gashmu saith it, that thou and the Jews think to rebel: for which cause thou buildest the wall, that thou mayest be their king, according to these words. And thou hast also appointed prophets to preach of thee at Jerusalem, saying, There is a king in Judah: and now shall it be reported to the king according to these words. Come now therefore, and let us take counsel together. Then I sent unto him, saying, There are no such things done as thou sayest, but thou feignest them out of thine own heart. For they all made us afraid, saying, Their hands shall be weakened from the work, that it be not done. Now therefore, O God, strengthen my hands.

Look at your hands. Are your hands weak? Have you been struggling? Have you been wondering to yourself, "Where in the world is God?" Have you been saying deep within your spirit, "God, I am so tired? I am so sick and tired of being tired. Where in the world are you now?" We have to learn that God has always been where God is. He has never moved. We are the ones that moved. When we move, God remains where He has always been, that is to say, waiting on us to come back to the place where He is. Determine now to come back to God. His door is always open. Enter once again into that warm and loving fellowship

71

you once knew with your Heavenly Father, The Lord God Almighty! The time is now. Return home today. Come home!

Prayer: Lord, I am coming home. I want to come home. I want to be with Thee. Thou art my everlasting hope. Thou art mine, dear Lord. I love Thee. I am coming home. I am coming home. Lord, I realize that is where the heart is, in Your Son, Jesus' Name, Amen!

Personalize Prayer: Write your own prayer, using A.C.T.S. Refer to The Journey's Preface for help.

_____

_____

_____

_____

_____

_____

_____

_____

_____

Prayer Journal Notes: Be honest and be real. Tell God what is going on right now in your life. Tell God just how you honestly feel. Are your hands weak? Do you need inner strength? Andrew Murray in his little book, *The Inner Life* says in the country of South Africa many diseases affect orange trees. One of them is root disease. A tree may be bearing fruit, and an ordinary observer may not notice anything wrong. However, an expert can see the beginning of a slow death. This disease also affects the vineyards, and there is only one cure found in recent days. That is to take out the old roots and provide new ones; then the gardener grafts the old vine onto the new root system. In time new stems, branches and fruit are as before, but the roots are newer and able to resist the disease. The gardener realizes that the disease comes in the part of the plant in places hidden from the human eye and that is where healing must also take place.

Murray goes on to say, "The Church of Christ and the spiritual life of thousands of its members suffer from root disease – the neglect of secret communion with God. Secret prayer once neglected inhibits the Christian life by limiting abundant fruitful productivity." Nothing can change this except the restoration of the inner chamber in the life of the believer. As Christians, we must learn to sink our roots deeper into Christ and to engage in a personal fellowship with God our main priority. Then, true godliness will flourish. "If the root be holy, so are the branches" (Romans 11:16). If we as disciples of the Lord Jesus Christ make the morning hour holy unto the Lord, the day with its duties will also be holy. If the root is healthy, the branches will be, too. Be honest, be real, and tell God about your "root disease" in order that He might strengthen your grip.

_____

_____

_____

_____

_____

_____

_____

_____

_____

**Pray all day for a God-sent revival in America.
Fast all day.**

DAY 8

JUSTICE PREVAILS

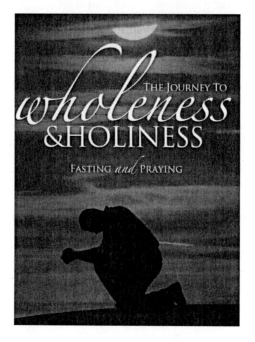

"Christians are not to be anxious or worried about anything,"

– James Montgomery Boice,
How to Live the Christian Life, p. 91.

Day 8

Justice Will Prevail

Read and Meditate: Habakkuk 1:2 – 4 (KJV)

O LORD, how long shall I cry, and thou wilt not hear! even cry out unto thee of violence, and thou wilt not save! Why dost thou shew me iniquity, and cause me to behold grievance? for spoiling and violence are before me: and there are that raise up strife and contention. Therefore the law is slacked, and judgment doth never go forth: for the wicked doth compass about the righteous; therefore wrong judgment proceedeth.

The journey to wholeness and holiness begins with a great deal of patience. I realize that in America we have what I call the microwave Christian. We want to nuke our spiritual lives to instantly become perfectly full-grown Christians. This is literally impossible. Great and mighty things take time to grow and mature. Time is often considered to be our best friends and it is equally considered to be our worst enemy. Every good thing takes time. There is no such thing as the microwave Christian.

I am so glad that God heard my cry. He did not allow me to rush the process of spiritual maturity. I refused to become a microwave Christian. I decided to be a gas-oven Christian. God is still working on me. One day I will be like Him. However, in the meanwhile, God still uses me for His good pleasure. "How long shall I cry, and thou wilt not hear! even cry out unto thee of violence, and thou wilt no save" (Hab. 1:2)! Despite such pain and pressure, justice prevails and I still refuse to become a microwave Christian. God wants us to be fully cooked and ready for service unto God and His people.

Prayer: Dear Lord Jesus, I am so impatient. I want things now. Help me to wait on Thee. Thou art mine, and I desire to learn how to wait. Lord, I will do nothing until you come. I will wait. Come, Lord Jesus. Come soon, in Jesus' name, Amen!

Personalize Prayer: Write your own prayer, using A.C.T.S. Refer to The Journey's Preface for help.

_____

_____

_____

_____

_____

_____

_____

_____

_____

_____

Prayer Journal Notes: Tell of those times when you got ahead of God and did your own thing. Tell the story, and God will bless you. Dietrich Bonhoeffer said, "When Christ calls a man, He bids him to come and die."[21] Remember, life in the Spirit always precedes death to self and the flesh. Tell it all. Tell God now.

_____

_____

_____

_____

_____

_____

_____

_____

_____

Pray for yourself.
Fast for one meal.

[21] Dietrich Bonhoeffer, *The Cost of Discipleship* (New York: Collier Books MacMillan Publishing Company, 1937, 1949, 1959, 1960, 1961, 1963), p. 7.

The Journey To Wholeness & Holiness

DAY 9

IF

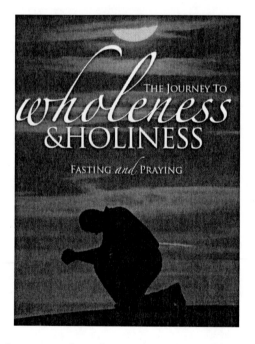

"God gives man time for communion with Himself."

— Andrew Murray, *An Exciting New Life*, p. 192.

Day 9

IF

Read and Meditate: 2 Chronicles 7:14 (KJV)

If my people, which are called by my name, shall humble themselves, and pray, and seek my face, and turn from their wicked ways; then will I hear from heaven, and will forgive their sin, and will heal their land.

How many of you realize that far too many Christians live in "The Kingdom of Ifdom?" If this happens, then I'll do this. If that happens, I will do that or the other. The call of God for every Believer is to move out of The Kingdom of Ifdom. However, this is something that just will not happen by simply speaking the words. You have to make up in your mind that this is not where you want to live anymore, because prayers prayed in The Kingdom of Ifdom never, get off the ground to "The Celestial Kingdom of God."

Do not be an "If" Christian. Become an "I can do" Christian, (Philippians 4:13). Humility requires prayer. We must pray our way out of "If – dom."

Prayer: Heavenly Father, I am moving out. I am moving out of The Kingdom of Ifdom. Help Lord. I pray. Help me please. This is your servant's prayer, in Jesus' Name, Amen!

Personalize Prayer: Write your own prayer, using A.C.T.S. Refer to The Journey's Preface for help.

_____

_____

_____

_____

_____

_____

_____

_____

_____

Prayer Journal Notes: Richard J. Foster's dynamic and most powerful work on prayer has truly helped me to get out of The Kingdom of Ifdom. In his book, *Prayer: Finding the Heart's True Home*, Foster says, "Prayer ushers us into the Holy of Holies, where we bow before the deepest mysteries of the faith, and one fears to touch the Ark" (p. xi). What are your "Ifs"? Are you still living in The Kingdom of Ifdom? Do you think that it is time for you to get out of Ifdom? Tell God the ways you feel that you need His help to get you out of The Kingdom of Ifdom.

_____

_____

_____

_____

_____

_____

_____

_____

_____

Pray for your immediate family members.
Fast 'til 12 o'clock midnight.

DAY 10

HE'S ABLE!

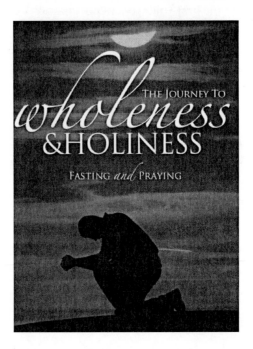

"Any truly repentant Christian has a right to full remission of penalty and guilt, even without indulgence letters."

– Martin Luther, *Ninety-five Theses.*

Day 10

God Is Able

Read and Meditate: Ephesians 3:14 – 21 (HCSB)

For this reason I bow my knees before the Father from whom every family in heaven and on earth is named. [I pray] that He may grant you, according to the riches of His glory, to be strengthened with power through His Spirit in the inner man, and that the Messiah may dwell in your hearts through faith. [I pray that] you, being rooted and firmly established in love, may be able to comprehend with all the saints what is the breadth and width, height and depth, and to know the Messiah's love that surpasses knowledge, so you may be filled with all the fullness of God. Now to Him who is able to do above and beyond all that we ask or think —according to the power that works in you — to Him be glory in the church and in Christ Jesus to all generations, forever and ever. Amen.

When we give our family tithes and offerings, this scripture passage is our family motto: "God is able."[22] I have come to learn that I can depend totally on God. God is indeed able. What is God able to do? He is able to do whatever He needs to do. The question that I want to ask each of us today is this. Are you willing to allow Him to be able? If you are not willing to allow Him to be able, then it will cancel His "ableness" for you. God will not force His will on us. Ask God to help you. He is able!

---

[22] Ephesians 3:20-21, NIV.

Prayer: Lord, you are able and I am not. But, today, I am willing to let you do as you please with me: Thank you, Lord. I love you with all my heart, in Jesus' name, Amen!

Personalize Prayer: Write your own prayer, using A.C.T.S. Refer to The Journey's Preface for help.

_____

_____

_____

_____

_____

_____

_____

_____

_____

Prayer Journal Notes: Os Guinness and John Seel made a powerful declaration, "No God But God."[23] If you are going to stay on the journey to wholeness and holiness then you too must make your declaration, "No God But God!" Tell what you are going to do as a faithful follower of Christ to let others know that your God is indeed able. Write it down. Then ask God for His divine assistance.

_____
_____
_____
_____
_____
_____
_____
_____
_____

Pray for your church.
Fast all day.

---

[23] Os Guinness and John Seel, _No God But God: Breaking with the Idols of Our Age_ (Chicago: Moody Press, 1992), p. 7.

Day 11

The Prayer of Jesus

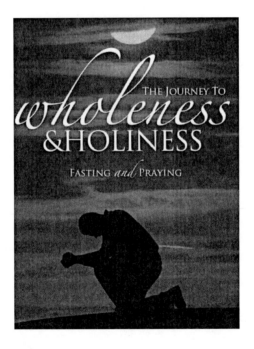

"Prayer is supposed to have an answer."

– Andrew Murray, *With Christ in the School of Prayer*, p. 31.

Day 11

When Jesus Prays, Part 1

Read and Meditate: John 17:1 – 5 (KJV)

These words spake Jesus, and lifted up his eyes to heaven, and said, Father, the hour is come; glorify thy Son, that thy Son also may glorify thee: As thou hast given him power over all flesh, that he should give eternal life to as many as thou hast given him. And this is life eternal, that they might know thee the only true God, and Jesus Christ, whom thou hast sent. I have glorified thee on the earth: I have finished the work which thou gavest me to do. And now, O Father, glorify thou me with thine own self with the glory which I had with thee before the world was.

Jesus knew how to pray. He was a prayer warrior. He had a connection to God that was indeed powerful and awesome. He was a man of prayer. His life demonstrated the heart and soul of His Heavenly Father, God, in "The Prayer of Jesus." He first prayed for Himself.

Prayer: Lord, I do not know how to pray like you, but if you would simply teach me, I know that would learn. Teach me dear Lord how to pray like you. I realize that you gave your disciples the Model Prayer in Matthew 6:9 – f.; however, I still need your help. Teach me Lord; teach me to pray like your Son, Jesus the Christ, in Jesus' Name, Amen!

Personalize Prayer: Write your own prayer, using A.C.T.S. Refer to The Journey's Preface for help.

_____

_____

_____

_____

_____

_____

_____

_____

_____

_____

Prayer Journal Notes: Richard J. Foster's work, *Prayer: Finding The Heart's True Home*, provides for us a litany of prayer types as vehicles to talk to God. In his wonderful ministry of prayer, Foster attempts to capture the very heart and soul of prayer, as he employs the heart of Christ, using the vehicle of "Simple Prayer." Foster describes Simple Prayer in the following passage.

> We bring ourselves before God just as we are, warts and all. Like Children before a loving father, we open our hearts and make our requests. We do no try to sort things out, the good from the bad. We simply and unpretentiously share our concerns and make our petitions. We tell God, for example, how frustrated we are with the co-worker at the office or the neighbor down the street. We ask for food, favorable weather, and good health.[24]

This is Simple Prayer. However, let us never forget that the Person of the Holy Spirit of God is still very active in the vehicle of Simple Prayer. So, simply tell God the place(s) where you find it difficult to pray. What problems are you having in your prayer life? Simply, tell God. He has at His fingertips a host of vehicles in His prayer shed to address our every need. Speak with Him in prayer. He's waiting on you.

_____
_____
_____
_____
_____
_____
_____

Pray for your pastor, his wife and his family
Fast 'til 5:00 p.m.

_____

[24] Foster, *Prayer*, p. 9.

DAY 12

THE PRAYER OF JESUS CONTINUES

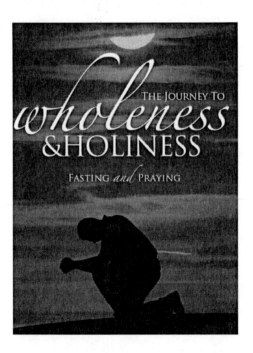

The vital connection between the Word and prayer is one of the simplest and earliest lessons of the Christian life."

– Andrew Murray, *With Christ in the School of Prayer*, p. 175.

Day 12

When Jesus Prays, Part 2

Read and Meditate: John 17:6 – 19   (HCSB)

I have revealed Your name to the men You gave Me from the world. They were Yours, You gave them to Me, and they have kept Your word. Now they know that all things You have given to Me are from You, because the words that You gave Me, I have given them. They have received them and have known for certain that I came from You. They have believed that You sent Me. I pray for them. I am not praying for the world but for those You have given Me, because they are Yours. All My things are Yours, and Yours are Mine, and I have been glorified in them. I am no longer in the world, but they are in the world, and I am coming to You. Holy Father, protect them by Your name that You have given Me, so that they may be one as We are one. While I was with them, I was protecting them by Your name that You have given Me. I guarded them and not one of them is lost, except the son of destruction, so that the Scripture may be fulfilled. Now I am coming to You, and I speak these things in the world so that they may have My joy completed in them. I have given them Your word. The world hated them because they are not of the world, as I am not of the world. I am not praying that You take them out of the world but that You protect them from the evil one. They are not of the world, as I am not of the world. Sanctify them by the truth; Your word is truth. As You sent Me into the world, I also have sent them into the world. I sanctify Myself for them, so they also may be sanctified by the truth.

95

Jesus now prays for His present disciples, and they really needed an abundance of prayer. Now let us be very careful. We need prayer in abundance as well. Never criticize others who are in need of prayer in abundance. Prayer is always welcome in any amount. We need this truth embedded in our prayer life as a lifestyle. What do you think will happen if we pray as Jesus prayed for one another? What do you think God will do even for a lonesome traveler?

Prayer: Heavenly Father, teach me how to pray for others. Teach me the power and the person of prayer. I want to pray with more power and more effectiveness. Teach me how to pray, in Jesus' Name, Amen!

Personalize Prayer: Write your own prayer, using A.C.T.S. Refer to The Journey's Preface for help.

_____

_____

_____

_____

_____

_____

_____

_____

_____

Prayer Journal Notes: In order for us as God's Children to have a powerful prayer life, we must learn how to be humble. We must learn what it means to "descend." In his book *Descending into Greatness,* Bill Hybels and Rob Wilkins tell us about the power of a humble heart, the kind of heart that Jesus possessed while on earth among men. No wonder God answered His prayers. Make a prayer list of people you feel God would have you pray for while on your personal journey. Now do not be self – righteous. You need prayer too. You are not that great either. We all need help. Now make your list and humbly pray for the persons on your list.

_____
_____
_____
_____
_____
_____
_____
_____
_____

Pray for our nation and leaders.
Fast for one meal.

The Journey To Wholeness & Holiness

DAY 13

THE PRAYER OF JESUS CLIMAX

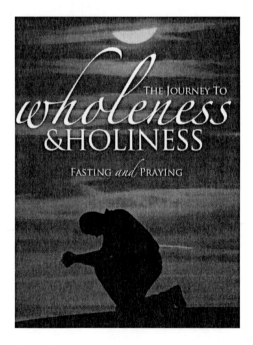

"God has instituted prayer so as to confer upon his creatures the dignity of being causes."

– Blaise Pascal, Richard J. Foster,
Prayer: Finding the Heart's True Home, p. 229.

Day 13

When Jesus Prays, Part 3

Read and Meditate: John 17:20 – 26 (KJV)

Neither pray I for these alone, but for them also which shall believe on me through their word; That they all may be one; as thou, Father, art in me, and I in thee, that they also may be one in us: that the world may believe that thou hast sent me. And the glory which thou gavest me I have given them; that they may be one, even as we are one: I in them, and thou in me, that they may be made perfect in one; and that the world may know that thou hast sent me, and hast loved them, as thou hast loved me. Father, I will that they also, whom thou hast given me, be with me where I am; that they may behold my glory, which thou hast given me: for thou lovedst me before the foundation of the world. O righteous Father, the world hath not known thee: but I have known thee, and these have known that thou hast sent me. And I have declared unto them thy name, and will declare it: that the love wherewith thou hast loved me may be in them, and I in them.

Now Jesus pauses to pray for all Believers. Are you glad that Jesus prayed for all of us? What would have happened, if Jesus refused to pray for sinful man? Where would we be if no one prayed for us? That is why we must pray always.

Prayer: Lord, I am ready to pray for the world. I am ready to pray for my friends, my family, and even my enemies. I am ready to pray. However, let me not pray a self – righteous prayer. Let me pray a humble prayer cradled in the grace and mercy of God's Agape (Love), in Jesus' Name, Amen!

Personalize Prayer: Write your own prayer, using A.C.T.S. Refer to The Journey's Preface for help.

_____

_____

_____

_____

_____

_____

_____

_____

_____

Prayer Journal Notes: When you make out this prayer list, pray for yourself as well. Admit it. We always stand in the need of prayer. Now make your new list, with you included. God bless you, for your faithfulness to the Lord God Almighty.

_____
_____
_____
_____
_____
_____
_____
_____
_____

Pray for a friend.
Fast 'til 12 o'clock midnight.

DAY 14

PRAYER AT MIDNIGHT

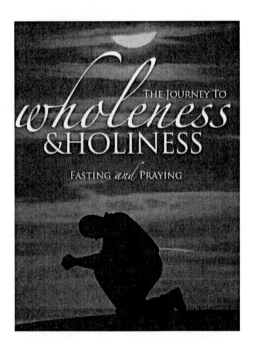

"Sanctification is both a step of faith and a process of works."

— Hannah Whitall Smith,
The Christian's Secret of a Happy Life, p. 17

Day 14

Answered Prayer At Midnight

Read and Meditate: Acts 16:25 – 34 (KJV)

And at midnight Paul and Silas prayed, and sang praises unto God: and the prisoners heard them. And suddenly there was a great earthquake, so that the foundations of the prison were shaken: and immediately all the doors were opened, and every one's bands were loosed. And the keeper of the prison awaking out of his sleep, and seeing the prison doors open, he drew out his sword, and would have killed himself, supposing that the prisoners had been fled. But Paul cried with a loud voice, saying, Do thyself no harm: for we are all here. Then he called for a light, and sprang in, and came trembling, and fell down before Paul and Silas, And brought them out, and said, Sirs, what must I do to be saved? And they said, Believe on the Lord Jesus Christ, and thou shalt be saved, and thy house. And they spake unto him the word of the Lord, and to all that were in his house. And he took them the same hour of the night, and washed their stripes; and was baptized, he and all his, straightway. And when he had brought them into his house, he set meat before them, and rejoiced, believing in God with all his house.

I remember waking up early in the wee hours of morning from a restless night sleep or being thirsty for a glass of water and hearing my mother praying. There were times when she was in complete tears. I did not understand why. I could sense her level of intensity. She appeared to be struggling with God. Her prayers often went like this, "Lord, help me with my kids. I don't know what to do with my kids. There are things they need. You know what I need to do.

105

Please help me, Heavenly Father, to do the right thing." My mom's prayers would go on and on and on.

I believe that this was so for Paul and Silas in their jail at Philippi. One sang and the other prayed. God answers prayer at midnight. God never sleeps. God is waiting on you and me to come to Him. It does not matter what we need. We can still talk to God, and because of that prayer meeting at midnight; salvation came to the jailer's household. His entire household got saved.

We do not know what our prayers can do. All we should do is just pray. Pray and seek the face and heart of God. God answers prayer. So, PUSH. Pray Until Something Happens. PUSH! PUSH! PUSH!

Prayer: Lord, I have been pushing for many years and nothing has happened. Is there something wrong with my prayers? What do I need to do to get you to answer my prayers? Lord, I believe I know what to do. Lord, I will continue to pray until you do your part. In addition, if you choose not to do anything at all, I will still pray. I will continue to PUSH – moreover, PUSH! PUSH! PUSH! Until you do whatever you wish.

Personalize Prayer: Write your own prayer, using A.C.T.S. Refer to The Journey's Preface for help.

_____

_____

_____

_____

_____

_____

_____

_____

_____

Prayer Journal Notes: Make a PUSH List, and keep on PUSHING! Keep on PUSHING until something happens. Now, jot down your PUSH List today.

_____

_____

_____

_____

_____

_____

_____

_____

_____

Pray for God to use you in a profound special way.
Fast for one hour (choose your time).

The Journey To Wholeness & Holiness

DAY 15

EARNEST PRAYER

"Unceasing Prayer has a way of speaking peace to the chaos."

– Richard J. Foster,
Prayer: Finding the Heart's True Home, p. 121.

Day 15

Earnest Prayer in The Church

Read and Meditate: Acts 12:5 – 18 (KJV)

Peter therefore was kept in prison: but prayer was made without ceasing of the church unto God for him. And when Herod would have brought him forth, the same night Peter was sleeping between two soldiers, bound with two chains: and the keepers before the door kept the prison. And, behold, the angel of the Lord came upon him, and a light shined in the prison: and he smote Peter on the side, and raised him up, saying, Arise up quickly. And his chains fell off from his hands. And the angel said unto him, Gird thyself, and bind on thy sandals. And so he did. And he saith unto him, Cast thy garment about thee, and follow me. And he went out, and followed him; and wist not that it was true which was done by the angel; but thought he saw a vision. When they were past the first and the second ward, they came unto the iron gate that leadeth unto the city; which opened to them of his own accord: and they went out, and passed on through one street; and forthwith the angel departed from him. And when Peter was come to himself, he said, Now I know of a surety, that the LORD hath sent his angel, and hath delivered me out of the hand of Herod, and from all the expectation of the people of the Jews. And when he had considered the thing, he came to the house of Mary the mother of John, whose surname was Mark; where many were gathered together praying. And as Peter knocked at the door of the gate, a damsel came to hearken, named Rhoda. And when

111

she knew Peter's voice, she opened not the gate for gladness, but ran in, and told how Peter stood before the gate. And they said unto her, Thou art mad. But she constantly affirmed that it was even so. Then said they, It is his angel. But Peter continued knocking: and when they had opened the door, and saw him, they were astonished. But he, beckoning unto them with the hand to hold their peace, declared unto them how the Lord had brought him out of the prison. And he said, Go shew these things unto James, and to the brethren. And he departed, and went into another place. Now as soon as it was day, there was no small stir among the soldiers, what was become of Peter.

Prayer is powerful. Prayer not only changes things, prayer changes the one who is praying. Peter was in prison. He was in trouble. Peter was sleeping between two soldiers, bound with two chains; sentries stood guard at the entrance, and then suddenly God showed up in the form of an angel. The angel touched Peter and before he could do anything, he was a free man. However, in the background, the Saints of God were praying. They were praying so hard and powerful until God answered their prayer while they were still praying. If it had not been for a little girl named Rhoda answering Peter's knock at the door, they would never have known that God had said, "Yes" to their prayers.

What most Christians fail to remember is this: Our responsibility is to pray, and it is God's job to respond to our prayer with "Yes," "No," or "Wait."

Prayer: Lord, I come to you today in prayer. Help me not to look up from my prayers. Help me to simply keep on praying until you do whatever you choose to do. Thank you Lord. I will be faithful in what I need to do. You are God, and you are God all by yourself, in Jesus' Name, Amen!

Personalize Prayer: Write your own prayer, using A.C.T.S. Refer to The Journey's Preface for help.

_____

_____

_____

_____

_____

_____

_____

_____

Prayer Journal Notes: Make a list of about twelve things that you had been praying for and before you knew it God had already answered. The journey to wholeness and holiness is always one of faith. Have faith in God Saints. Have faith in God! He will not let you down. He loves you so very much. You are His. You are His chosen people.

_____

_____

_____

_____

_____

_____

_____

_____

_____

Pray for pastoral leadership.
Fast for one meal.

The Journey To Wholeness & Holiness

DAY 16

IN THE FISH BELLY

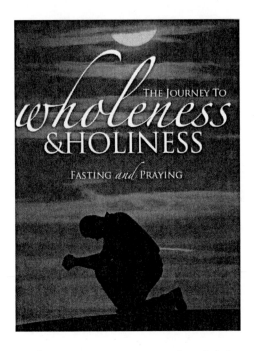

"No man-made gauge can measure the shock and horror
that strike the nervous system as ill-fated news
travels into the human ear."

– Charles R. Swindoll, *Seasons of Life*, p. 91.

Day 16

A Prayer Meeting in the Belly of a Fish

Read and Meditate: Jonah 2:1 – 10 (KJV)

Then Jonah prayed unto the LORD his God out of the fish's belly, And said, I cried by reason of mine affliction unto the LORD, and he heard me; out of the belly of hell cried I, and thou heardest my voice. For thou hadst cast me into the deep, in the midst of the seas; and the floods compassed me about: all thy billows and thy waves passed over me. Then I said, I am cast out of thy sight; yet I will look again toward thy holy temple. The waters compassed me about, even to the soul: the depth closed me round about, the weeds were wrapped about my head. I went down to the bottoms of the mountains; the earth with her bars was about me for ever: yet hast thou brought up my life from corruption, O LORD my God. When my soul fainted within me I remembered the LORD: and my prayer came in unto thee, into thine holy temple. They that observe lying vanities forsake their own mercy. But I will sacrifice unto thee with the voice of thanksgiving; I will pay that that I have vowed. Salvation is of the LORD. And the LORD spake unto the fish, and it vomited out Jonah upon the dry land.

What a strange place to have a prayer meeting. Who would ever have thought that you could have church in the belly of a big fish? Jonah prayed and God answered. The journey to wholeness and holiness occurs in strange and unusual places. God put Jonah in the fish's belly and God got Jonah out too. And when Jonah got out, he was ready to do whatever God wanted him to do.

Prayer: Lord, please do not let me be like Jonah. Lord, I am ready to do whatever you want me to do. Lord, it does not take the belly of a big fish to get my undivided attention. Lord, I am ready to do your bidding. Lord, I am yours, in Jesus' Name, Amen!

Personalize Prayer: Write your own prayer, using A.C.T.S. Refer to The Journey's Preface for help.

_____

_____

_____

_____

_____

_____

_____

_____

_____

Prayer Journal Notes: In your journal, write about your time in the belly of a big fish. Tell how and when God allowed you to come out.

_____

_____

_____

_____

_____

_____

_____

_____

_____

Pray five times today for yourself.
Fast all day.

DAY 17

LOOK LIKE CHRIST

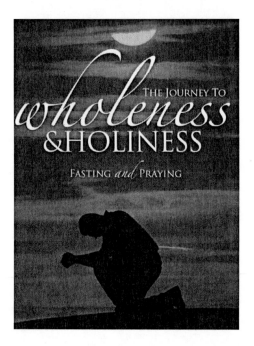

"The earnestness that we work up in the energy of the flesh
is a repulsive thing. The earnestness created in us
by the Holy Spirit if pleasing to God."

– R. A. Torrey, *Power-Filled Living: How to Receive God's
Best for Your Life*, p. 290.

Day 17

Learning to Look Like Christ

Read and Meditate: Ephesians 5:1 – 2 (HCSB)

*Therefore, be imitators of God, as dearly loved children.
And walk in love, as the Messiah also loved us and gave
Himself for us, a sacrificial and fragrant offering to God.*

It is good to look like Christ. To imitate Christ is the goal of every Believer. This is how one knows divine ownership. When we imitate Christ, we are telling the world that we belong to Almighty God. Do you belong to God? Do you imitate Christ? Do people refer to you as a Child of God? Whose child are you?

Prayer: Lord, I want to be more and more like you, Lord. Make me like you, Lord. I want to be just like you.

> Lord I want to be a Christian, in my heart, in my heart. Lord I want to be a Christian, in my heart. In my heart, in my heart …Lord I want to be a Christian, in my heart. Lord I want to be more holy, in my heart, in my heart. Lord I want to be more holy, in my heart. In my heart, in my heart …Lord, I want to be a Christian, in my heart.[25]

In Jesus' Name, Amen!

Personalize Prayer: Write your own prayer, using A.C.T.S. Refer to The Journey's Preface for help.

_____
_____
_____
_____
_____
_____
_____
_____
_____

---

[25] T. B. Boyd, III, *National Baptist Hymnal*, "Lord I Want To Be A Christ" (Nashville: National Baptist Publishing Board, 1981, 8th Edition), p. 490.

Prayer Journal Notes: In your journal tell when you felt that you were doing your very best imitating of Christ. Do you remember the most recent time?

_____
_____
_____
_____
_____
_____
_____
_____
_____

Pray all day for college and university students to do well. Fast all day.

DAY 18

MATURING ON THE JOURNEY

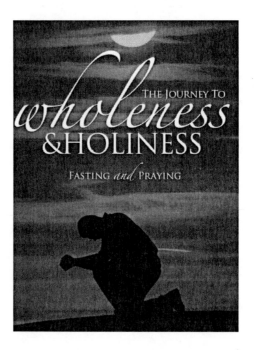

"Unfortunately, blind spots affect more than cars.
All of us have personal blind spots."

– Bill McCartney, *Blind Spots*, p. 7.

Day 18

Maturing on the Journey to Wholeness & Holiness

Read and Meditate: Ephesians 4:14 – 16 (HCSB)

> *Then we will no longer be little children, tossed by the waves and blown around by every wind of teaching, by human cunning with cleverness in the techniques of deceit. But speaking the truth in love, let us grow in every way into Him who is the head — Christ. From Him the whole body, fitted and knit together by every supporting ligament, promotes the growth of the body for building up itself in love by the proper working of each individual part.*

The journey to wholeness and holiness requires growing up. You cannot remain a child. You must desire to grow up. Infantile religion is not going to do it. You must grow up!

Upward growth also requires humility. Jesus said, in Matthew 18, "Become as little children." It is when we are like little children, that God matures us. This is known as the journey inward and downward into the secret places of our inner being. Only He knows where that place is.

Maturity is always a matter of responding to His choice. Bible teachers call such responding to this certainty "human free will." We have the free will to surrender to growing up into Christ. This is maturity at its best.

There is an expression that is often said, "You are the linchpin between the explosive conflict between man's free will and God's perfect will." God is the initiator. He came to seek and to save the lost. Jesus saves. We are in Christ. We desire to live as mature Christians. This is operating in the perfect will of God and not in His permissive will. Do you know the difference between the perfect will of God and the permissive will of God? God's perfect will implies what God prefers for us, while God's permissive will implies what God permits us to do. Perfect will – Divine Choice. Permissive will – Divine Allowance. Like a loving parent, God will not force His perfect will on us as His Children. Therefore, mature Christians on the journey to wholeness and holiness, seek to know God's perfect will.

Prayer: Lord, I want to mature. I no longer want to act like a kid. I want to grow up and mature. I want to be all that you would have me to be and do, in Jesus' Name, Amen!

Personalize Prayer: Write your own prayer, using A.C.T.S. Refer to The Journey's Preface for help.

_____

_____

_____

_____

_____

_____

_____

_____

_____

Prayer Journal Notes: Write a note to yourself, expressing your appreciation of how you have grown. For an example: Dear Pastor, "I am so proud of you. You have truly grown in the LORD, etc."

_____

_____

_____

_____

_____

_____

_____

_____

_____

Pray all day for little boys and girls who need adoption. Fast 'til 5:00 p.m.

The Journey To Wholeness & Holiness

DAY 19

BE REAL

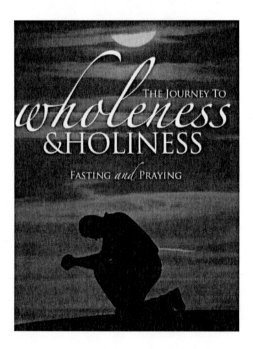

"What's the cure for selfishness? Get your self out of your eye by getting your eye off your self. Quit staring at that little self, and focus on your great Savior."

– Max Lucado, *Grace for the Moment*, Vol. II, p. 30.

Day 19

Be Real And Speak the Truth

Read and Meditate: Ephesians 4:25 (HCSB)

Since you put away lying, Speak the truth, each one to his neighbor, because we are members of one another.

The time has come for you and me to put off falsehood and speak truthfully to our neighbor. This is how you know that you are maturing. What a joy to see you grow in the power of the person of the Lord Jesus Christ. Are you growing every day? This is what God wants for all of His children. It is time to grow up and be a truth speaker in love. Jesus said, "Ye shall know the truth, and the truth shall make you free."[26] Jesus also said on another occasion, "I am the way, the truth, and the life: no man cometh unto the Father, but by me."[27] Jesus frequently parallels truth and freedom, which leads to deliverance and being real. Paul is right on target, "...put away lying, Speak the truth, each one to his neighbor, because we are members of one another."

---

[26] John 8:32, KJV.
[27] John 14:6, KJV.

Prayer: Lord, I want to be real and truthful in all that I do. Will you help me, Father, to do it the way you would have me to? Lord, I am your child. Will you teach me Lord? Will you teach me to do as you please, in Jesus' Name, Amen?

Personalize Prayer: Write your own prayer, using A.C.T.S. Refer to The Journey's Preface for help.

_____

_____

_____

_____

_____

_____

_____

_____

_____

Prayer Journal Notes: Write in your journal when you had to speak truthfully to your brother or your sister. Then write in your journal when your brother or sister had to speak truthfully to you. Jot it down and be blessed!

_____
_____
_____
_____
_____
_____
_____
_____
_____

Pray all day for pastors to preach the Word of God. Fast for one meal.

DAY 20

BE ANGRY, SIN NOT

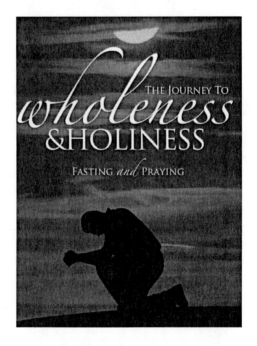

"Portraits of hurt will be replaced by landscapes of grace.
Walls of anger will be demolished and
shaky foundations restored."

– Max Lucado, *Everyday Blessings*, p. 276.

Day 20

Be Angry But Sin Not

Read and Meditate: Ephesians 4:26 – 27 (HCSB)

Be angry and do not sin. Don't let the sun go down on your anger, and don't give the Devil an opportunity.

June Hunt is one of the best Christian writers that I have read on dealing with anger. Anger is not bad. It becomes bad when it is not under the control of the Holy Spirit of God. God tells us that we can be angry but we should not sin. God wants to use our anger to glorify Him. That is why Paul said, "In your anger do not sin." If you are a person of anger, take it all to God. He will heal and help you overcome your problem with the spirit of anger. God is waiting to hear from you. Ask His help, and He will help you.

Don't let your anger lure you in missing God's best for you and your life. You have a wonderful life ahead of you. You don't have to continue to live frustrated trying to suppress the flame within you. You know what I'm talking about. You know that you are an angry person.

Are you afraid to admit your anger? Are you ashamed of your countless outbursts? Are you disappointed in your uncontrollable, ungodly, un-Christian-like explosive outbursts? Do you feel helpless? Do you need help? Do you feel like it's hopeless?

Don't give up. God is still at work. He knows what you need. He understands your unveiled frustrations and shame. God is ready to help you, my brother or my sister. God knows what you need. He is simply waiting on you to

135

request assistance. Listen to His loving words, "Don't let the sun go down on your anger. In other words, you have the power to change right now." God has placed changing power at your fingertips. Changing power is resting on the tip of your tongue. My brother or my sister, reach out and open up your mouth and lift up your voice to God and say, "I don't want to live a life in changeless anger. Lord, help me. I'm ready to change. I want to change now."

Do you really mean what you are saying? Are you sincerely ready to embrace changing power? If you are indeed ready for changing power, then listen to what I honestly believe is God's response.

"Since you have asked, I will give you the desire of your heart. As your heavenly Father, I seek to grant you gifts of all kinds to help you achieve what's always best for you my son or my daughter. Your request has been granted. Relax. You are now freed from the furnace of volcanic molten anger."

Now what should you do when God liberates you from years of an unchanged life, spurring out red-hot coals of smoldering anger at anybody and everybody at random? I believe you ought to fall on your knees right where you are and genuinely express gratitude to God.

Prayer: Pray this prayer. "Dear Lord, I am a person filled with so much anger. Heal me Lord. Please, Father, heal me. I want to be made whole. I do not want to continue to live like this. I need healing, in Jesus' Name, Amen!"

Personalize Prayer: Write your own prayer, using A.C.T.S. Refer to The Journey's Preface for help.

_____

_____

_____

_____

_____

_____

_____

_____

_____

Prayer Journal Notes: In your Journal, tell how God is helping you with your anger, and if you are not a person who deals with outward expressions of anger, then tell how God is teaching you how to use your anger for His glory.

_____
_____
_____
_____
_____
_____
_____
_____
_____

Pray all day for our government and president.
Fast 'til 5:00 p.m.

The Journey To Wholeness & Holiness

DAY 21

BE HONEST

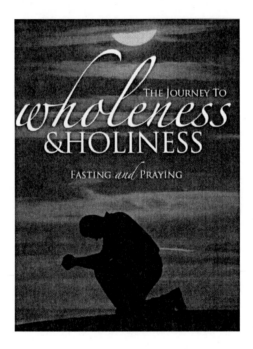

"God wants more than slavish obedience from us, He wants
to change us…G. K. Chesterton once wrote, 'Virtue is not
just the absence of vices or the avoidance of moral dangers;
virtue is a vivid and separate thing.'"

– Terry Glaspey, *C. S. Lewis: His Life & Thoughst*, p. 124.

Day 21

Be Honest & Don't Steal

Read and Meditate: Ephesians 4:28 (HCSB)

The thief must no longer steal. Instead, he must do honest work with his own hands, so that he has something to share with anyone in need.

Don't be a thief. Don't steal. Stealing is a sin. Be honest. Being honest is very good. God can use you best when you are honest and truthful before God and man. This is Godly character at its best, because you are a child of God.

As a child of God, you want to demonstrate Christ is in all that you do and say. God knows that we are not perfect; yet, He still commands us to be like Him. What makes us honest and truthful people? What keeps us from stealing and lying? What makes us unlike the culture of this age? John sheds a ray of light on Paul's words to the Ephesians' Christian community. John tells us to abide in Him. "If ye abide in me, and my words abide in you, ye shall ask what ye will, and it shall be done unto you. Herein is my Father glorified, that ye bear much fruit; so shall ye be my disciples."[28] Attach your life to Christ. Abide in Him, and you will be honest and you will not steal.

---

[28] John 15:7-8, KJV.

Prayer: Lord, would you please make me more like you? I want more of you and less of me, in Jesus' Name, Amen!

Personalize Prayer: Write your own prayer, using A.C.T.S. Refer to The Journey's Preface for help.

_____

_____

_____

_____

_____

_____

_____

_____

_____

_____

Prayer Journal Notes: In your journal, write about the times when God had to humble you. Then write about the times when God exalted you unexpectedly.

_____

_____

_____

_____

_____

_____

_____

_____

_____

**Pray three times for someone you know personally.
Fast 'til 12 o'clock midnight.**

DAY 22

MOUTH CLEANING

"He who has a sharp tongue soon cuts his own throat."

– E. C. McKenzie, *Quips & Quotes*, p. 518.

Day 22

Clean Out Your Mouth

Read and Meditate: Ephesians 4:29 (HCSB)

No rotten talk should come from your mouth, but only what is good for the building up of someone in need, in order to give grace to those who hear.

The tongue is a very powerful instrument. God wants us as Christians to use our tongues with great wisdom and understanding. The Scriptures says, "Do not let any unwholesome talk come out of your mouths…" God is not telling us to stop talking and having fun. He is simply telling us to be careful what we say to others. James says,

> *Don't be in any rush to become a teacher, my friends. Teaching is highly responsible work. Teachers are held to the strictest standards. And none of us is perfectly qualified. We get it wrong nearly every time we open our mouths. If you could find someone whose speech was perfectly true, you'd have a perfect person, in perfect control of life. A bit in the mouth of a horse controls the whole horse. A small rudder on a huge ship in the hands of a skilled captain sets a course in the face of the strongest winds. A word out of your mouth may seem of no account, but it can accomplish nearly anything—or destroy it! It only takes a spark, remember, to set off a forest fire. A careless or wrongly placed word out of your mouth can do that. By our speech we can ruin the world, turn harmony to chaos, throw mud on a reputation, send the whole world up in smoke and go up in smoke with*

it, smoke right from the pit of hell. This is scary: You can tame a tiger, but you can't tame a tongue—it's never been done. The tongue runs wild, a wanton killer. With our tongues we bless God our Father; with the same tongues we curse the very men and women he made in his image. Curses and blessings out of the same mouth! My friends, this can't go on. A spring doesn't gush fresh water one day and brackish the next, does it? Apple trees don't bear strawberries, do they? Raspberry bushes don't bear apples, do they? You're not going to dip into a polluted mud hole and get a cup of clear, cool water, are you?[29]

We as Christians need to be very careful how we use our tongues. The tongue is like a razor. It cuts and it hurts. We want to use our tongues as Christians to build up the body of Christ, as God would have it. As Christians, we believe in the power of the tongue. The Christian tongue is an encouraging tongue, truth-speaking tongue, loving tongue, praising tongue, exhorting tongue, a spirit-filled tongue and most of all a saved tongue. Jesus provides tongue management. This is the grace of God at its best, Jesus!

---

[29] James 3:1-12, *The Message*, Copyright © 1993, 1994, 1995, 1996, 2000, 2001, 2002 by Eugene H. Peterson.

Prayer: Lord, as I open my mouth, praise, exaltations and worship of your holy and righteous name. I want you to take my tongue and use it for God's glory, in Jesus' name, Amen!

Personalize Prayer: Write your own prayer, using A.C.T.S. Refer to The Journey's Preface for help.

_____

_____

_____

_____

_____

_____

_____

_____

_____

Prayer Journal Notes: Tell God how you plan to use your tongue for the next several days as you continue *The Journey To Wholeness & Holiness.*

_____
_____
_____
_____
_____
_____
_____
_____
_____

Pray one hour (choose the time).
Fast for one meal.

The Journey To Wholeness & Holiness

DAY 23

FORGIVE

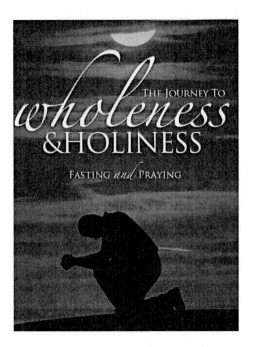

"Violence is the ugliest fruit."

— Max Lucado, *A Love Worth Giving*
Living in the Overflow of God's Love, p. 38.

Day 23

Be Kind to Each Other & Forgive in Christ

Read and Meditate: Ephesians 4:32 (HCSB)

And be kind and compassionate to one another, forgiving one another, just as God also forgave you in Christ.

The fruit of forgiveness is kindness and compassion. God forgives us; let us forgive one another as well. If you do not forgive, then do not expect God to forgive you. Jesus taught His disciples how to pray. He prayed,

> *And when you pray, do not be like the hypocrites, for they love to pray standing in the synagogues and on the street corners to be seen by others. Truly I tell you, they have received their reward in full. But when you pray, go into your room, close the door and pray to your Father, who is unseen. Then your Father, who sees what is done in secret, will reward you. And when you pray, do not keep on babbling like pagans, for they think they will be heard because of their many words. Do not be like them, for your Father knows what you need before you ask him. This, then, is how you should pray: Our Father in heaven, hallowed be your name, your kingdom come, your will be done, on earth as it is in heaven. Give us today our daily bread. And forgive us our debts, as we also have forgiven our debtors. And lead us not into temptation, but deliver us from the evil one. For if you forgive others when they sin against you, your heavenly Father will also*

151

forgive you. But if you do not forgive others their sins, your Father will not forgive your sins.[30]

Go and stand in front of your bathroom mirror and speak these words from your heart, "I forgive you for hurting me." God bless you for your obedience. You are now free. "So if the Son sets you free, you will be free indeed."[31]

---

[30] Matthew 6:5-15, *Today's New International Version (TNIV)* © Copyright 2001, 2005 by International Bible Society.
[31] John 8:35, "True Freedom," NIV.

Prayer: Dear Lord, I have been deeply hurt, by many people, but today I forgive and release them to you, in Jesus' name, Amen!

Personalize Prayer: Write your own prayer, using A.C.T.S. Refer to The Journey's Preface for help.

_____
_____
_____
_____
_____
_____
_____
_____
_____

Prayer Journal Notes: Think of a situation in which you have been deeply hurt by another person. Now, ask God these questions. "Have I truly forgiven my offenders? Am I free? Am I healed deep within the inner most parts of my creative being?" If not, then repeat this prayer for the next seven days until the Spirit of God enables you to do it. "Lord, I now give the forgiveness you gave to me to my offenders, in Jesus' name, Amen!"

_____

_____

_____

_____

_____

_____

_____

_____

_____

Pray all day for people who need medical care.
Fast all day.

The Journey To Wholeness & Holiness

DAY 24

LIVE AGAPE

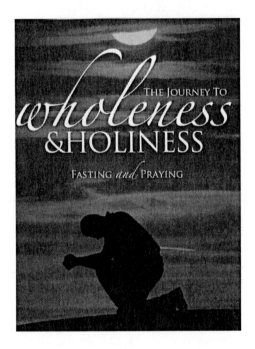

"The rebellious slogan 'All for love' is really love's death warrant (date of execution, for the moment, left blank)."

– C. S. Lewis, *The Four Loves*, pp. 166-167.

Day 24

Our Goal is to Imitate Jesus Christ to Live Agape

Read and Meditate: Ephesians 5:2 (HCSB)

And walk in love, as the Messiah also loved us and gave Himself for us, a sacrificial and fragrant offering to God.

Live Agape! What does it mean to Live Agape? Living Agape means to live a life of love. Christian love is agape. Christ provided us with this kind of love. It is unconditional, despite our faults, failures, and fallen human condition. I am so glad that Christ loves me in this manner. How do you feel about this? Do you realize just how much Christ loves you too? You are His creation and He really loves you. That is why Paul cried out, "...and live a life of love, just as Christ loved us and gave himself up for us as a fragrant offering and sacrifice to God." Love is eternally expensive and sacrificially costly. Authentic agape love requires blood, the blood of Jesus. Love died on a cross for the sins of the world. Love is our hope and grace. G.R.A.C.E.! What is it? God's Riches At Christ's Expense, that's G.R.A.C.E. That is why grace is so amazing. It's "Amazing Grace." The Ancient of Days is the giver of grace.

In Judaism, the Ancient of Days appears three times in the Bible in the book of Daniel 7:9, 13 and 22, and is used in the sense of God being eternal. In contrast with all earthly kings, God's days are past reckoning.[32]

---

[32] "Ancient of Days," *Wikipedia Encyclopedia.*

In Christianity, the Ancient of Days in Eastern Orthodox Christian hymns and icons, the Ancient of Days is sometimes identified with God the Father, and sometimes with God the Son, or Jesus Christ. As such, an icon will sometimes portray Jesus Christ as an old man, the Ancient of Days, to show symbolically that he existed from all eternity, and sometimes as a young man to portray him as he was incarnate. In the hymn "Immortal, Invisible, God only Wise," the last two lines of the first verse read: Most blessed, most glorious, the Ancient of Days, Almighty, victorious, Thy great Name we praise. The Ancient of Days is also the name of a painting by William Blake, that great English poet of old.[33]

Grace is God giving me His favor, when I do not deserve it; whereas, mercy is God not giving me what I deserve, even though, I have earned it. Romans 5:6-8 tells us,

> *When we were utterly helpless, Christ came at just the right time and died for us sinners. Now, most people would not be willing to die for an upright person, though someone might perhaps be willing to die for a person who is especially good. But God showed his great love for us by sending Christ to die for us while we were still sinners.[34]*

---

[33] Ibid.

[34] Romans 5:6-8, "God's Timing," *New Living Translation (NLT)* Holy Bible, 1996, 2004.

All of this is at the loving hand of the Ancient of Days. He expresses His love with the symbol of the cross and an empty tomb. We call this in Christianity, the Resurrection.[35]

---

[35] 1 Corinthians 15:50-f., "The Resurrection of Jesus Christ," gives us victory over death, hell and the grave. As God's people, we have absolute victory.

Prayer: Father, I want to personally thank you for your wonderful, amazing grace. Lord, please don't give me justice. Lord, please give me grace, in Jesus' name, Amen!

Personalize Prayer: Write your own prayer, using A.C.T.S. Refer to The Journey's Preface for help.

_____

_____

_____

_____

_____

_____

_____

_____

_____

Prayer Journal Notes: What has God done for you lately? Write in your journal about an amazing grace experience you've had with God. Then stop and praise Him for all the things He has done on your behalf.

_____
_____
_____
_____
_____
_____
_____
_____
_____

Pray all day for people in need of reliable transportation. Fast all day.

Day 25

House Cleaning Time

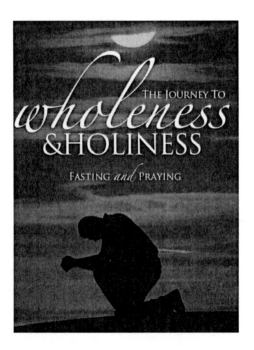

"Hatred has its pleasures. It is therefore often
the compensation by which a frightened man reimburses
himself for the miseries of Fear.
The more he fears, the more he will hate."

– C. S. Lewis, *The Screwtape Letters*, p. 136

Day 25

It's House Cleaning Time: Clean up Your Hearts

Read and Meditate: Ephesians 5:3 – 6 (HCSB)

But sexual immorality and any impurity or greed should not even be heard of among you, as is proper for saints. And coarse and foolish talking or crude joking are not suitable, but rather giving thanks. For know and recognize this: no sexually immoral or impure or greedy person, who is an idolater, has an inheritance in the kingdom of the Messiah and of God.

      The Apostle Paul spoke to the heart of the early Christians in his letter to the Ephesians. However, many years ago, like the Ephesians, King David had a heart problem too. He had sinned against God and man. What did King David do with his sin? He sought God's forgiveness. The king repented before the throne of the King of kings, the LORD God Almighty. In Psalm 51, we can see clearly David's repentant heart:

O God, favor me because of Your loving-kindness. Take away my wrong-doing because of the greatness of Your loving-pity. Wash me inside and out from my wrong-doing and make me clean from my sin. For I know my wrong-doing, and my sin is always in front of me. I have sinned against You, and You only. I have done what is sinful in Your eyes. You are always right when You speak, and fair when You judge. See, I was born in sin and was in sin from my very

163

beginning. See, You want truth deep within the heart. And You will make me know wisdom in the hidden part. Take away my sin, and I will be clean. Wash me, and I will be whiter than snow. Make me hear joy and happiness. Let the bones that You have broken be full of joy. Hide Your face from my sins. And take away all my wrong-doing. Make a clean heart in me, O God. Give me a new spirit that will not be moved. Do not throw me away from where You are. And do not take Your Holy Spirit from me. Let the joy of Your saving power return to me. And give me a willing spirit to obey you. Then I will teach wrong-doers Your ways. And sinners will turn to You. Save me from the guilt of blood, O God. You are the God Who saves me. Then my tongue will sing with joy about how right and good You are. O Lord, open my lips, so my mouth will praise You. For You are not happy with a gift given on the altar in worship, or I would give it. You are not pleased with burnt gifts. The gifts on an altar that God wants are a broken spirit. O God, You will not hate a broken heart and a heart with no pride. Be pleased to do good to Zion. Build the walls of Jerusalem. Then You will be happy with gifts given on the altar that are right and good, with burnt gifts and whole burnt gifts. Then young bulls will be given on Your altar.[36]

King David sought mercy; however, God's mercy found him, and God restored him. God wants to do the very same for you as well. Let Him do it for you today. If you need restoration, come back to God: Come back now!

---

[36] Psalm 51, "David's Confession of Sin," *New Life Version (NLV),* 1969.

Prayer: Lord, I'm coming home. I want to start over again. Help me, dear Lord. I am ready to let you have your way, in Jesus' name, Amen!

Personalize Prayer: Write your own prayer, using A.C.T.S. Refer to The Journey's Preface for help.

_____

_____

_____

_____

_____

_____

_____

_____

_____

Prayer Journal Notes: Read Psalm 51 and meditate on it. Ask God to give you divine insight into God's heart. Now prayerfully write in your journal what God has revealed to you as to what is the relationship between Psalm 51 (David's Heart) and Ephesians 5:3 – 6 (Paul's Heart).

_____

_____

_____

_____

_____

_____

_____

_____

_____

Pray all day for families and people in debt.
Fast all day.

The Journey To Wholeness & Holiness

DAY 26

A LIFE CHANGE

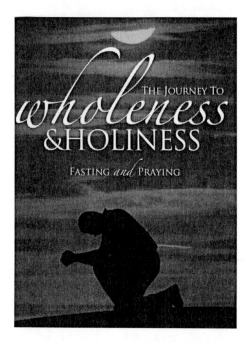

"What you see and hear depends a good deal on where you are standing: it also depends on what sort of person you are."

– C. S. Lewis, *The Magician's Nephew*, p. 125.

Day 26

There has been a Change in My Life

Read and Meditate: Ephesians 5:8 – 10 (KJV)

For ye were sometimes darkness, but now are ye light in the Lord: walk as children of light: (For the fruit of the Spirit is in all goodness and righteousness and truth;) Proving what is acceptable unto the Lord.

Jesus wants us to be children of light. He does not want us to live in darkness. Darkness means death. Light means life. Darkness is a life away from God. Light is a life in the very presence of God. Which one do you want: Light or Darkness? The choice is up to you. What are you going to do?

Jesus said that there is a way to live with the right type of attitude: the "Beatitudes!" Christian teaching reveals that the Beatitudes teach us to walk in the light of God and thus become both salt and light.[37] That is what we need to be to complete the journey to wholeness and holiness.

And seeing the multitudes, he went up into a mountain: and when he was set, his disciples came unto him: And he opened his mouth, and taught them, saying, Blessed are the

---

[37] "Salt and light" is one of the many expressions, Jesus employs in His teaching in the Gospels. Jesus referred to those who sincerely embraced His teaching as being like "salt and light." Salt was symbolic of preserving, whereas "light" was the converse of darkness and death. Therefore, changed life people were those who were both "salt and light" a sinful, dying and fallen world.

poor in spirit: for theirs is the kingdom of heaven. Blessed are they that mourn: for they shall be comforted. Blessed are the meek: for they shall inherit the earth. Blessed are they which do hunger and thirst after righteousness: for they shall be filled. Blessed are the merciful: for they shall obtain mercy. Blessed are the pure in heart: for they shall see God. Blessed are the peacemakers: for they shall be called the children of God. Blessed are they which are persecuted for righteousness' sake: for theirs is the kingdom of heaven. Blessed are ye, when men shall revile you, and persecute you, and shall say all manner of evil against you falsely, for my sake. Rejoice, and be exceeding glad: for great is your reward in heaven: for so persecuted they the prophets which were before you. Ye are the salt of the earth: but if the salt have lost his savour, wherewith shall it be salted? it is thenceforth good for nothing, but to be cast out, and to be trodden under foot of men. Ye are the light of the world. A city that is set on an hill cannot be hid. Neither do men light a candle, and put it under a bushel, but on a candlestick; and it giveth light unto all that are in the house. Let your light so shine before men, that they may see your good works, and glorify your Father which is in heaven.[38]

Be blessed! Be light! Be salt! Be Whole! Be Holy! Be all that God would have you to be! Be saved! Be set free! It is possible through Christ. God wants you to be lighthouses for His glory! So, Shine!

---

[38] Matthew 5:1-16, "The Beatitudes and Beyond," (KJV).

Prayer: Father, I realize that I am not what I need to be. So, take me as I am and make me what you would have me to be. I know that you can. I know that you will, in Jesus' Name, Amen!

Personalize Prayer: Write your own prayer, using A.C.T.S. Refer to The Journey's Preface for help.

_____

_____

_____

_____

_____

_____

_____

_____

_____

Prayer Journal Notes: In your journal, tell when God used you in a mighty way. Then, pause and praise God for doing that in your life.

_____

_____

_____

_____

_____

_____

_____

_____

_____

**Pray all day for teen mothers and teen fathers.
Fast 'til 5:00 p.m.**

The Journey To Wholeness & Holiness

DAY 27

LORD, HELP!!!

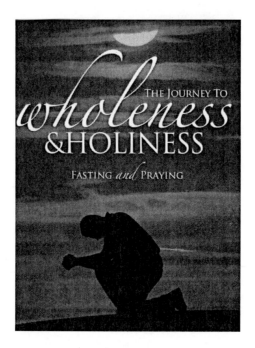

"You've seen your Godzilla.
The question is, is he all you see?"

– Max Lucado, *Facing Your Giants*, p. 4.

Day 27

Dear Lord, Help Me get the Junk Out of My Heart

Read and Meditate: Ephesians 5:11 – 14 (KJV)

And have no fellowship with the unfruitful works of darkness, but rather reprove them. For it is a shame even to speak of those things which are done of them in secret. But all things that are reproved are made manifest by the light: for whatsoever doth make manifest is light. Wherefore he saith, Awake thou that sleepest, and arise from the dead, and Christ shall give thee light.

What Paul is saying to us is, that we can change. Change is what we need to do every day; change reveals God's glory at its best. "Surface Christianity" is not an expression of the depth of the heart of God. You must go deeper. Going deeper does not suggest intellectualism; it suggests realism. This makes "spiritual realism" authentic. Spiritual realism precedes salvation. You must be born again. Jesus said to Nicodemus, "Marvel not that I said unto thee, Ye must be born again."[39] It's time for a change. Paul said, "You can still change."

---

[39] John 3:7 speaks of "The Necessity of the New Birth," KJV.

Prayer: Lord, change me now! Make me what you want me to be. I am ready. Do it, LORD! Do it now, please, in Jesus' Name, Amen!

Personalize Prayer: Write your own prayer, using A.C.T.S. Refer to The Journey's Preface for help.

_____

_____

_____

_____

_____

_____

_____

_____

_____

Prayer Journal Notes: In your notes, tell how God has changed you. Focus on a few things that have changed in your life in recent days.

_____
_____
_____
_____
_____
_____
_____
_____
_____

Pray all day for sick babies.
Fast for two meals.

DAY 28

LIVING WISE

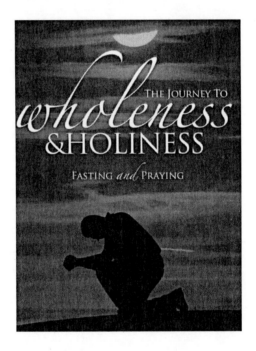

"Those who wish to succeed must
ask the right preliminary questions."

– Aristotle, Metaphysics, II, (III), I,
C. S. Lewis, *The Complete C. S. Lewis
Signature Classics*, p. 303.

Day 28

Wise Living

Read and Meditate: Ephesians 5:15 – 16 (KJV)

See then that ye walk circumspectly, not as fools, but as wise, Redeeming the time, because the days are evil.

Are you careful how you live your life, or are you living your life just any old way? The wise man lives his life with great wisdom. How are you living your life? Are you a wise woman or man? Are you a wise young woman or young man? Are you a wise teenager? What do you think God would say about you right now? He would say, "If any man needs wisdom, he should ask God, who gives it liberally."[40] Paul said,

Where is the wise? where is the scribe? where is the disputer of this world? hath not God made foolish the wisdom of this world? [21] For after that in the wisdom of God the world by wisdom knew not God, it pleased God by the foolishness of preaching to save them that believe.[41]

We must live wisely.

---

[40] James 1:5.
[41] 1 Corinthians 1:20-21, "We Need Godly Wisdom For The Journey," KJV.

Prayer: Father, I have a need for greater wisdom. You said, I could ask you for more wisdom. That is what I need. Fill me with Godly wisdom and not just the wisdom of the world, in Jesus' Name, Amen!

Personalize Prayer: Write your own prayer, using A.C.T.S. Refer to The Journey's Preface for help.

_____
_____
_____
_____
_____
_____
_____
_____
_____

Prayer Journal Notes: In your notes, what is the difference between man's wisdom and God's wisdom? Do you know the difference? Explain!

_____
_____
_____
_____
_____
_____
_____
_____
_____

Pray all day for people who are on death row.
Fast 'til 12 o'clock midnight.

DAY 29

MOVING FROM... TO

"Christianity helps us face the music,
even when we don't like the tune."

– E. C. McKenzie, *Quips & Quotes*, p. 173.

Day 29

Moving from Foolishness to Faithfulness

Read and Meditate: Ephesians 5:17 – 18 (KJV)

Wherefore be ye not unwise, but understanding what the will of the Lord is. And be not drunk with wine, wherein is excess; but be filled with the Spirit...

You should never mix foolishness with faith. Paul says, to each of us, *"be filled with the Spirit of the Living God."* When God fills you up, you will be totally filled. Do you want God to fill you up? The mark of a foolish man or woman is empty words uttered by a foolish mouth. Jesus said, in Matthew 12,

> *...for out of the overflow of the heart the mouth speaks. The good man brings good things out of the good stored up in him, and the evil man brings evil things out of the evil stored up in him. But I tell you that men will have to give account on the day of judgment for every careless word they have spoken. For by your words you will be acquitted, and by your words you will be condemned."[42]*

This is a word to the wise. Keep your words as few as possible. As you open your mouth to speak, ask God to project a visible image of every word projected through the projector of your soul that beams through the lens of your lips, rolling off the fleshly tape of your tongue words you

---

[42] Matthew 12:34-37, "Keep Your Words Few," NIV.

have often uttered foolishly without a thought in mind, for words that you learn to use habitually even when you know you are wrong.

It is time for you to move. It is time for you to relocate from living foolishly to living faithfully. God is waiting to help you. Ask Him and He will come to your rescue.

Prayer: Dear Jesus, I am in need of a fill up! Fill me with all of you and none of me, in Jesus' Name, Amen!

Personalize Prayer: Write your own prayer, using A.C.T.S. Refer to The Journey's Preface for help.

_____
_____
_____
_____
_____
_____
_____
_____
_____

Prayer Journal Notes: In your notes, tell how God revealed to you personally some foolish things in your life.

_____

_____

_____

_____

_____

_____

_____

_____

_____

_____

Pray all day for people in prison.
Fast for one meal.

The Journey To Wholeness & Holiness

DAY 30

THE LANGUAGE OF LOVE

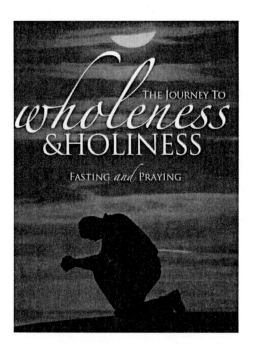

The Great Sin: "For Pride is spiritual cancer:
it eats up the very possibility of love, or contentment,
or even common sense."

– C. S. Lewis, *Mere Christianity*, p. 97.

Day 30

Learning How to Use the Language of Love

Read and Meditate: Ephesians 5:19 – 20 (HCSB)

...speaking to one another in psalms, hymns, and spiritual songs, singing and making music to the Lord in your heart, giving thanks always for everything to God the Father in the name of our Lord Jesus Christ...

Speaking to people is not an art, but rather, it is about a Christian heart. When you speak to others with your heart and not with your head, God does "something supernatural." What do I mean by the supernatural? Andrew Murray defines the something supernatural as being an invitation into the inner life. The inner life is where the heart of the language of love originates. It is the birthplace of child-like love introduced to the world in the person of a child wrapped in swaddling clothes cradled in a manger. Something supernatural is an invitation into the inner life. Murray humbly writes,

> The daily need for a time of solitude and quiet to pray and read God's Word is of utmost importance. This time spent in fellowship with God will bring a blessing, strengthen our spiritual life, and prepare us to meet the world. Then, we will be equipped for service in God's Kingdom in soul-winning and intercession.[43]

---

[43] Andrew Murray, *Inner Life* (Springdale: Whitaker House, 1984), p. 5.

This is inner life. It is a journey inward to learn how to use the language of love. This is the goal of every disciple of the Lord Jesus Christ to learn how to speak with your heart and not with your head.

> *Jesus said, O generation of vipers, how can ye, being evil, speak good things? for out of the abundance of the heart the mouth speaketh. A good man out of the good treasure of the heart bringeth forth good things: and an evil man out of the evil treasure bringeth forth evil things. But I say unto you, That every idle word that men shall speak, they shall give account thereof in the day of judgment. For by thy words thou shalt be justified, and by thy words thou shalt be condemned.[44]*

---

[44] Matthew 12:34-37, "*How do you know a man's heart? Simply, listen to his mouth and he will tell you his heart.*" (KJV).

Prayer: Father, my heart wants to speak. Please, Heavenly Father, will you teach me the heart language of love. This is a language beyond the words of the head. Thank you for helping me to do as you command, in Jesus' Name, Amen!

Personalize Prayer: Write your own prayer, using A.C.T.S. Refer to The Journey's Preface for help.

_____

_____

_____

_____

_____

_____

_____

_____

_____

Prayer Journal Notes: In your journal, tell some stories of how you have spoken to people from your head as opposed to your heart.

_____
_____
_____
_____
_____
_____
_____
_____
_____

**Pray all day for your church family and yourself.
Fast all day for unity in God's church family.**

The Journey To Wholeness & Holiness

DAY 31

BIBLICAL SUBMISSION

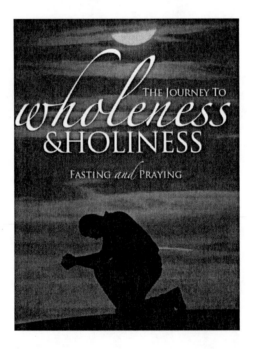

The Great Sin: "If you think you are not conceited, it means you are very conceited indeed."

– C. S. Lewis, *Mere Christianity*, p. 99.

Day 31

The Submitting Family, Part 1, Biblical Submission

Read and Meditate: Ephesians 5:21 (HCSB)

...Submitting to one another in the fear of Christ.

In a Biblically submitted home, there is peace, love, joy, compassion and sincere warmth. But in a non-Biblically submitted home, there is pain, suffering and war on every hand. Biblical submission knows no gender. It is bother for Adam and Eve to genuinely submit to one another out of love. That is why, authentic Biblical submission emanates from the holy heart of God.

The word for Biblical submission is "hupotassso." Hupotasso is a Greek New Testament term, often used to express a military idea, meaning, "to rank under." "Hupo" means "under," and "tasso," means "to arrange."[45] Hupotasso suggests the arranging of oneself under in subjection to a superior source. Submit first to God and He will lift you up. You cannot ascend, until you descend. Descending requires humble obedience to a power greater and mightier than your power. This power is El Shaddai, "God Almighty." Submit to His power! If you fail to do so, you will not be willing to submit to one another in reverence to Christ. Christians revere Christ. If you really want order

---

[45] "Subjection, or Subject", *Hupotasso*, W. E. Vine, *Vine's Complete Expository Dictionary of the Old and New Testament Words* (Nashville: Thomas Nelson Publishers, 1996), 606.

in your home, first get things right with God. If things are not right with God, then do not expect things to be right with others. God: First! Man: Second! This is the proper Biblical order.

Prayer: Lord, I feel that my life is out of order. Things are just not right. Life for me is out of order. I need your help. I want to be in order, in Jesus' Name, AMEN!

Personalize Prayer: Write your own prayer, using A.C.T.S. Refer to The Journey's Preface for help.

_____

_____

_____

_____

_____

_____

_____

_____

_____

Prayer Journal Notes: In your journal, tell how you realized that your life was out of order, and how God helped you to move toward a more orderly life in Christ.

_____
_____
_____
_____
_____
_____
_____
_____
_____

Pray all day for marital submission in our homes.
Fast all day for us as husbands and wives to learn how to submit one to the other.

The Journey To Wholeness & Holiness

DAY 32

THE SUBMITTING WIFE

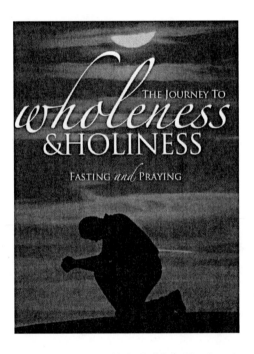

The Great Sin: "The utmost evil, is Pride. Unchastity, anger, greed, drunkenness, and all that, are mere fleabites in comparison: it was through Pride that the devil became the devil: Pride leads to every other vice: it is the complete anti-God state of mind."

– C. S. Lewis, *Mere Christianity*, p. 94.

Day 32

The Submitting Family, Part 2, Wives

Read and Meditate: Ephesians 5:22 – 24 (HCSB)

Wives, submit to your own husbands as to the Lord, for the husband is head of the wife as also Christ is head of the church. He is the Savior of the body. Now as the church submits to Christ, so wives should [submit] to their husbands in everything.

A wife must submit to Christ first. If she refuses to submit to Christ, she will not be in loving submission to her husband, who is the head of the wife as Christ is the head of the church. Proper Biblical order in marital relationships demands obedience to headship. Is your relationship with your husband out of order? Do you need order in your marital relationship? Do you have order in the house? If you do not have order in your house, start with submission to Christ Jesus today and order will come into your house, immediately. Immediately the Spirit driveth him into the wilderness.[46] Immediately his fame spread abroad throughout the entire region round about Galilee.[47] Immediately the fever left her, and she ministered unto them.[48] As soon as he had spoken, immediately the leprosy departed from him, and

---

[46] Mark 1:12, KJV.
[47] Mark 1:28, KJV.
[48] Mark 1:31, KJV.

he was cleansed.[49] Immediately he received his sight, and followed Jesus in the way.[50] Immediately means right now!

The word "immediate" in the Gospel of Mark is the word Greek New Testament word "euthus." The word euthus coveys a message of urgency in that God never waste time responding to us in a time of human crisis and we should do likewise when it comes to immediate obedience to the will of God. Immediate obedience enhances marital faithfulness and happier home. Beverly LaHaye calls this act of immediate obedience the Spirit-controlled life. In her masterful book, *The New Spirit-Controlled Woman*, Beverly LaHaye admits she was still missing something in her spiritual life while attending a Christian conference at Forest Home, California, in 1963. She said and I quote:

> I heard Dr. Henry Brandt, a Christian psychologist and speaker; give a message about the filling of the Holy Spirit and the effect it could have on a life that fully surrendered to the Holy Spirit. Although the Holy Spirit dwells in a believer's heart at the moment of salvation, the filling of the Holy Spirit is when a believer completely submits to the Holy Spirit. This was the first time it had been presented to me so clearly, and I came face-to-face with the realization that this filling was a missing dimension in my life.[51]

Immediate obedience is always connected to living a spirit filled life in Christ. When this happens the prideful spirit of superiority is given over to the humble spirit of submission. Euthus!

---

[49] Mark 1:42, KJV.
[50] Mark 10:52, KJV.
[51] Beverly LaHaye, *The New Spirit-Controlled Woman* (Eugene Oregon: Harvest House Publishers, 1995/2005), p. 13.

Prayer: Dear Lord, I want order. I am ready to seek improvement in my marriage. I am ready for a better life with my husband, dear Lord, in Jesus' Name, Amen!

Personalize Prayer: Write your own prayer, using A.C.T.S. Refer to The Journey's Preface for help.

_____

_____

_____

_____

_____

_____

_____

_____

_____

Prayer Journal Notes: Journal as to what happened to you as you submitted to God before submitting to your husband, in Jesus' Name!

_____
_____
_____
_____
_____
_____
_____
_____
_____

Pray all day for aging, confused parents.
Fast all day.

The Journey To Wholeness & Holiness

DAY 33

THE SUBMITTING HUSBAND

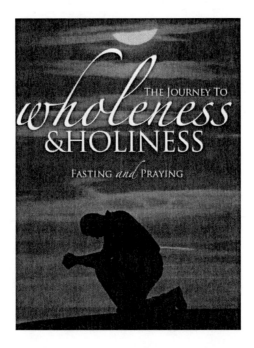

The Great Sin: "As long as you are proud you cannot know God. A proud man is always looking down on things and people: and, of course, as long as you are looking down, you cannot see something that is above you."

– C. S. Lewis, *Mere Christianity*, p. 96.

Day 33

The Submitting Family, Part 3, Husbands

Read and Meditate: Ephesians 5:25 – 33 (HCSB)

Husbands, love your wives, just as also Christ loved the church and gave Himself for her, to make her holy, cleansing her in the washing of water by the word. He did this to present the church to Himself in splendor, without spot or wrinkle or any such thing, but holy and blameless. In the same way, husbands should love their wives as their own bodies. He who loves his wife loves himself. For no one ever hates his own flesh, but provides and cares for it, just as Christ does for the church, since we are members of His body. For this reason a man will leave his father and mother and be joined to his wife, and the two will become one flesh. This mystery is profound, but I am talking about Christ and the church. To sum up, each one of you is to love his wife as himself, and the wife is to respect her husband.

The husband is to love his wife just as Christ loves the church. This is a high order. The husband should not expect his wife to submit to him, if he doesn't submit to Christ first. Brother, submit first to Christ and watch your home become a haven. Do you want peace in your home? Do you want peace with your wife? Do you want a better life? Submit to Christ today and watch God work on your behalf. Submit now!

Prayer: Dear Lord, I am a man. I am not a boy. I am ready to be blessed. I submit to you, Christ. I submit, in Jesus' Name, Amen!

Personalize Prayer: Write your own prayer, using A.C.T.S.
Refer to The Journey's Preface for help.

_____

_____

_____

_____

_____

_____

_____

_____

_____

Prayer Journal Notes: Tell how you were led to submit to Christ. Tell what happened to your home thereafter, and most importantly; tell how you and your spouse are now living for God's glory.

_____

_____

_____

_____

_____

_____

_____

_____

_____

Pray all day for hungry people.
Fast all day.

DAY 34

SUBMITTING CHILDREN

The Great Sin: "The vain persons wants praise, applause, admiration, too much and is always angling for it."

– C. S. Lewis, Mere Christianity, p. 97

Day 34

The Submitting Family, Part 4, Children

Read and Meditate: Ephesians 6:1 – 3 (HCSB)

Children, obey your parents in the Lord, because this is right. Honor your father and mother —which is the first commandment with a promise — that it may go well with you and that you may have a long life in the land.

Children admonished to obey parental authority were perfect examples of proper Christian behavior. This is a good thing. However, most adults want their cake and eat it too. Far too many adults want to be youthful, yet at the same time grown. There is nothing wrong with being youthful; however, the problem is when we as adults refuse to grow up and become mature. When adults remain childlike, delayed adolescence is the outcome. In this world, the age of an adult does not always imply maturity. Mature Christians assume responsibility willingly and joyfully.

Therefore, why should a child submit to another child? This simply does not make good common sense. Someone needs to be the adult. I hope that the adult would be the adult and the child would be the child and obey his/her parents for God's glory. Why is this so important today? It is because this is right. "Honor your father and mother – which is the first commandment with a promise." What is the promise? The Bible promises, long life. The promise of long life is the product of a surrendered life. What is a surrendered life? A surrendered life is a life of absolute obedience to God. R. A. Torrey, says, "God floods the heart of the believer who surrenders absolutely to Him with light and joy and fills his life with power. Absolute surrender to God is the secret of blessedness and power."[52] God is a promise keeper and He will keep His promises. Live now and forever more absolutely surrendered to God, and you will never be put to shame as you honor your parents. Remember, the promise is for you.

---

[52] R. A. Torrey, *Power-Filled Living: How To Receive God's Best For Your Life* (New Kensington, PA: Whitaker House, 1998), p. 69.

Prayer: Dear Lord, my (or our) kids need Thee. I (or we) also need Thee as parents as well. I (or we) am (or are) in deep water with our kids. Help! Help me (or us) to do a better job in raising my (our) kids, in Jesus' Name, Amen! If you are a kid, pray for your parents. Ask God to help them in being your parents, in Jesus' Name, Amen!

Personalize Prayer: Write your own prayer, using A.C.T.S. Refer to The Journey's Preface for help.

_____

_____

_____

_____

_____

_____

_____

_____

_____

Prayer Journal Notes: Tell what you feel your kids need. And if you are a kid, tell God what you need.

_____
_____
_____
_____
_____
_____
_____
_____
_____

Pray all day for the building of the Lord's church. Fast all day.

The Journey To Wholeness & Holiness

DAY 35

SUBMITTING
FATHERS

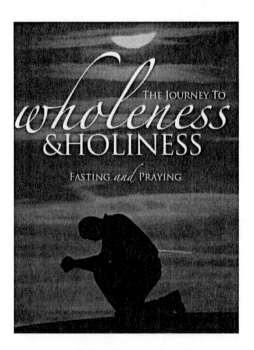

The Great Sin: "Pride always means enmity – it is enmity.
And not only enmity between man and man,
but enmity to God,"

– C. S. Lewis, *Mere Christianity*, p. 96.

Day 35

The Submitting Family, Part 5, Fathers

Read and Meditate: Ephesians 6:4 (HCSB)

And fathers, don't stir up anger in your children, but bring them up in the training and instruction of the Lord.

Fathers where are you today? Families profoundly need dads. They cannot make it without the purposeful participation of the fathers. Dad, you are needed. Where are you?

Paul did not hesitate to say, "don't stir up anger in your children." When I read this, I had to stop and think a while. I began to ask myself a few questions. Have I ever gone too far in disciplining my kids? Have I chastened them in anger? Do I regret it? Yes, I regret being too hard on kids. I have failed far more times than I would like to admit. I have not always been the best example of a Godly dad, but I refuse to give in and give up. As long as breath remains in my body, I will not give up! I will continue to do my very best to do what is righteous with my two sons. It is not an easy thing! It is truly a challenge. I need God's help!

Prayer: My heavenly Father, Dad! I'm a dad too. I need you to help me to do right about my kids. I have been wrong far too many times to count. I can't do this on my own. Help me, Lord. Help me please. Dad, my Heavenly Father, help me stay focused in my prayer life as an earthly father to bless my sons and daughters. Finally, dear Lord, I want to humbly bow and pray for all dads.

Personalize Prayer: Write your own prayer, using A.C.T.S. Refer to The Journey's Preface for help.

_____

_____

_____

_____

_____

_____

_____

_____

_____

Prayer Journal Notes: What does the word father mean to you?

_____
_____
_____
_____
_____
_____
_____
_____
_____
_____

**Pray all day for the building of the Lord's church.
Fast all day.**

DAY 36

SUBMITTING WORKERS

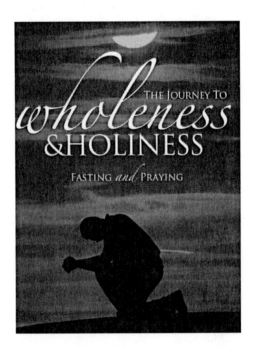

The Great Sin: "The real test of being in the presence of God
is that you either forget about yourself altogether
or see yourself as a small, dirty object.
It is better to forget about yourself altogether."

– C. S. Lewis, *Mere Christianity*, pp. 96-97.

Day 36

The Submitting Family, Part 6, Employees/Employers

Read and Meditate: Ephesians 6:5 – 9 (HCSB)

Slaves, obey your human masters with fear and trembling, in the sincerity of your heart, as to Christ. Don't [work only] while being watched, in order to please men, but as slaves of Christ, do God's will from your heart. Render service with a good attitude, as to the Lord and not to men, knowing that whatever good each one does, slave or free, he will receive this back from the Lord. And masters, treat them the same way, without threatening them, because you know that both their and your Master is in heaven, and there is no favoritism with Him.

New Testament understanding of the word "slave" is an invitation to life. We are to be slaves for Christ. The Greek New Testament word for slave is the word "doulos." A doulos is a bond slave. He/she is under the complete control of his/her master. A doulos does only what the master commands. The doulos and the master-teacher relationship rest on simple obedience. To live a successful and meaningful life unto God requires living the life of a slave and being under the guidance and direction of the master. The master is God, and He is in essence the Master or the Rabbi of the universe. He is worthy of our praise and faithful service. He is God's Son, Jesus Christ.

Prayer: If you are an employer, pray for your employees. If you are an employee, pray for your employer.

Personalize Prayer: Write your own prayer, using A.C.T.S. Refer to The Journey's Preface for help.

_____

_____

_____

_____

_____

_____

_____

_____

_____

_____

Prayer Journal Notes: Tell how you feel about your employee or your employer. Then ask God to help you become a better employee or employer: Ask God to help you become a better Christian.

_____
_____
_____
_____
_____
_____
_____
_____
_____

Pray all day for the saving of souls.
Fast for two meals.

DAY 37

GOD'S DRESS CODE

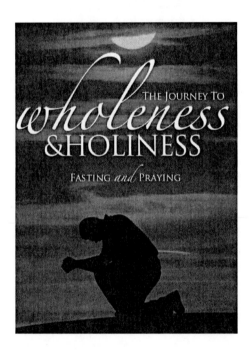

"Gospel peace lifts the Believer above danger."

– William Gurnall,
The Christian in Complete Armour, Vol. 2, p. 388.

Day 37

God's Dress Code: Put on the Full Armor of God

Read and Meditate: Ephesians 6:10 – 17 (HCSB)

Finally, be strengthened by the Lord and by His vast strength. Put on the full armor of God so that you can stand against the tactics of the Devil. For our battle is not against flesh and blood, but against the rulers, against the authorities, against the world powers of this darkness, against the spiritual forces of evil in the heavens. This is why you must take up the full armor of God, so that you may be able to resist in the evil day, and having prepared everything, to take your stand. Stand, therefore, with truth like a belt around your waist, righteousness like armor on your chest, and your feet sandaled with readiness for the gospel of peace. In every situation take the shield of faith, and with it you will be able to extinguish the flaming arrows of the evil one. Take the helmet of salvation, and the sword of the Spirit, which is God's word.

Today we are improperly dressed. Some of us have lost our shoes, while others are still looking in the basement for our sword, which is the Word of God. We must be ready for the battle. If not, then why are you and I not ready? I contend that many of us do not believe that He's coming back. May I speak for myself, I believe time is coming to an end, and we must be ready and not just get ready. The time is now!

Prayer: Dear Lord, I want to be properly dressed for battle. Dress me, Lord with the kind of armor I truly need for the battle, in Jesus' Name, Amen!

Personalize Prayer: Write your own prayer, using A.C.T.S. Refer to The Journey's Preface for help.

_____

_____

_____

_____

_____

_____

_____

_____

_____

Prayer Journal Notes: Tell what armor you need to have repaired for the battle with the Evil One.

_____

_____

_____

_____

_____

_____

_____

_____

_____

Pray all day for homeless children.
Fast all day.

DAY 38

GOD'S SPIRIT

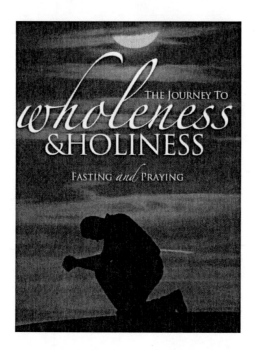

"True prayer is prayer offered to God the Father on the basis
of the death of Jesus Christ, his Son."

– James Montgomery Boice,
How to Live the Christian Life, p. 20.

Day 38

God's Divine Communication: Prayer in the Spirit

Read and Meditate: Ephesians 6:18 (HCSB)

With every prayer and request, pray at all times in the Spirit, and stay alert in this, with all perseverance and intercession for all the saints.

Mature Christians understand that prayer is key in communicating with God. When is the right time to pray? Paul, the Apostle to the Gentiles, said, "all times" is the right time, but how then should we pray? Paul goes on to add, "in the Spirit." However, why is Spirit-anointed prayer at such a high premium? Once again, the text gives us the answer. It is necessary for us to "stay alert in this, with all perseverance and intercession for all the saints." Why do we say "all the saints?" Can the Saints pray for themselves? Yes! However, there is even greater power when believers join in collective prayer. God then unleashes a more profound level of power. This is what happened in Acts 2. The believers prayed and something happened. And it was called Pentecost!

We are in need of holiness and wholeness. We need a visit from the Supernatural. We need divine intervention; however, this will not happen until there is a bended knee and a bowed down head and a broken and submissive heart open to God's divine instructions. When this happens, the Spirit of God will do the rest. PRAY! PRAY NOW! PRAY HARD! God answers prayers

Prayer: Dear Lord, make me a person of prayer. I want to not only know how to pray but also what to pray for in difficult times. Help me become a more effective person of prayer, in Jesus' Name, Amen!

Personalize Prayer: Write your own prayer, using A.C.T.S. Refer to The Journey's Preface for help.

_____

_____

_____

_____

_____

_____

_____

_____

_____

Prayer Journal Notes: A.C.T.S.: First there is "Adoration," second this is "Confession," third there is "Thanksgivings" and finally there is "Supplication (which means "to stand in the gap" and pray on the behalf of others)." An Example of an A.C.T.S. Prayer: *Adoration* – "Lord we adore Thee. You are an awesome God." *Confession* – "Lord I have sinned and fallen short of your glory. Please forgive me, Lord. I am so sorry." *Thanksgivings* – "Dear Lord, I just want to thank you for all that you have done for me. You have been so good to me, and I know that I don't deserve all of your goodness." *Supplication* – "Dear Lord, I'm standing in the gap for my kids, my husband, my wife, my home, my boss, my friends, my church family etc."

_____

_____

_____

_____

_____

_____

_____

_____

Pray all day for lonely singles.
Fast all day.

DAY 39

DEEP, DEEP LOVE

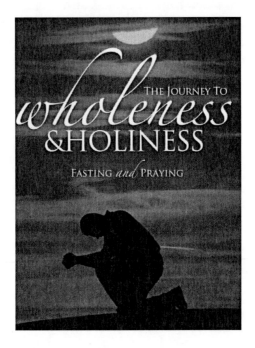

"Love of the brethren arises from the love of the Father."

– Andrew Murray, *An Exciting New Life*, p. 77.

Day 39

God's Deep Love: Pray for One Another

Read and Meditate: Ephesians 6:18 – 20 (HCSB)

With every prayer and request, pray at all times in the Spirit, and stay alert in this, with all perseverance and intercession for all the saints. Pray also for me, that the message may be given to me when I open my mouth to make known with boldness the mystery of the gospel. For this I am an ambassador in chains. Pray that I might be bold enough in Him to speak as I should.

I have often wondered to myself, "How deep is the Love of God for all of us earthbound folks?" I would simply love to know. I can say one thing, "I know that it is deep!" This is deep love! Love One Another" as Christ has loved us all with deep love, agape love, the deepest of all loves. This love persevered in all situations, hardships, pain, suffering, and the like. I must say, I have been blessed to know pain. What a blessing it is to serve the Lord twenty-four seven pain free, amidst painful blessing. What is twenty-four seven? Twenty-four seven implies, 24 hours a day and 7 days a week. God is love! God is present. This is such a wonderful reality. God Loves His children! What a wonderful thing! Praise the Name of the Lord Jesus Christ.

Prayer: Stop and pray for one another in Jesus' Name, Amen!

Personalize Prayer: Write your own prayer, using A.C.T.S. Refer to The Journey's Preface for help.

_____

_____

_____

_____

_____

_____

_____

_____

_____

Prayer Journal Notes: Make a prayer list of people you are praying for on a daily basis.

_____
_____
_____
_____
_____
_____
_____
_____

Pray all day for wounded-hearted people.
Fast all day.

DAY 40

GODLY DETERMINATION

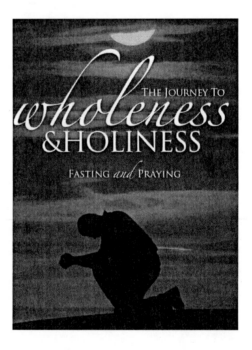

"When Mr. Steadfast had thus set things in order, and time being come for him to haste there was a great calm at that time in the River...."

– John Bunyan, *The Pilgrim's Progress*, p. 377.

Day 40

God's Determination: Peace to the Brothers And Sisters

Read and Meditate: Ephesians 6:21 – 24 (HCSB)

Tychicus, our dearly loved brother and faithful servant in the Lord, will tell you everything so that you also may know how I am and what I'm doing. I am sending him to you for this very reason, to let you know how we are and to encourage your hearts. Peace to the brothers, and love with faith, from God the Father and the Lord Jesus Christ. Grace be with all who have undying love for our Lord Jesus Christ.

Determination is our family's motto. We simply believe God in all situations. When things are hard, we believe God. When things appear impossible, we still believe God. When we cannot see our way clear, we remain committed to believe God. We have concluded as a family, that there are ways, but there is only one best and right way and that is the way of the cross of the Lord Jesus Christ. Isaiah said, "But he was wounded for our transgressions, he was bruised for our iniquities: the chastisement of our peace was upon him; and with his strips we are healed."[53] Thank you Lord, I am healed!

However, divine healing is really what we need. Divine healing requires pardon from sin. Jesus came to deliver men from sin and sickness so that He might make known the love of His heavenly Father for us as sinful creatures in this rebellious culture. Jesus makes people well. His ministry is one of peaceful and productive inner healing.

---

[53] Isaiah 53:5, KJV, "Christ of God, Our Sacrificial Lamb."

This is the peaceful healing of man's sin-sick soul. Andrew Murray calls such peaceful healing, "pardon from sin."[54] God literally forgives us of our blatant sinful rebellion.

Although, God does not turn His head from our sin, He simply wills His righteous judgment upon human sin in the form of the cross. The cross of Jesus Christ, cast a loving redemptive shadow of crimson blood that flowed beyond the pit of sinful rebellion, where there is no peace, only to provide hope, help and eternal healing. I am so glad that God refused to give up on me. His determination, determined my eternal destiny.

---

[54] Andrew Murray, *Divine Healing* (New Kensington, PA: Whitaker House, 1982), p. 10.

Prayer: Dear Lord, I need your peace. I know that you are the source all pure peace. Give me that peace, in Jesus' Name, Amen!

Personalize Prayer: Write your own prayer, using A.C.T.S. Refer to The Journey's Preface for help.

_____

_____

_____

_____

_____

_____

_____

_____

_____

Prayer Journal Notes: Tell how you know that you have perfect peace in your life; however, if for some reason or another you don't have perfect peace, then pray and ask God to give it to you.

_____
_____
_____
_____
_____
_____
_____
_____
_____

Pray all day for fearful children and single parents.
Fast all day.

The Journey To Wholeness & Holiness

The Journey To Wholeness & Holiness

PEAKS AND VALLEYS

REFLECTIONS

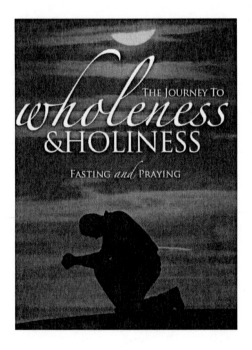

Concluding The 40 Days
Peaks And Valleys
Reflections

Congratulations!!! You have made it. You have completed your journey. Your commitment level has been awesome. You are to be praised for a job well done. However, you are not finished. Why? The Christian is never completely whole or holy until the day we see Jesus face-to-face. It will be a glorious day when our Lord and Savior Jesus Christ returns. I can't wait to be there with you and all of my fellow travelers on the Christian journey. What a day of rejoicing it will be.

Now let's turn our attention to the conclusion of our journey. I call this section "Peaks and Valleys".[55] What I would like for you to do is to take about thirty minutes and pause to reflect over your journey to wholeness and holiness. What did God say to you? What things did you see and/or experienced during your journey? Did you experience some deep changes in your life? Were you challenged to live more obediently to God? What peaks did you soar to? What valleys did you descend into? What did you learn about yourself and your personal relationship to Almighty God?

This is your opportunity to do a little introspective prodding. You may be surprised as to what you will find once you begin to turn over a few rocks and stones in your life that have been covered for years. Now, roll up your sleeves, grit your teeth and press pen or pencil to paper and write. Go for it. Give it all you've got. You have nothing to

---

[55] In the journey to wholeness and holiness, equanimity identifies the travelers' success despite peaks and valleys. Therefore peaks and valleys is the epitome of each traveler perspective on the journey to wholeness and holiness. The Lord God is the master of peaks and valleys.

243

lose. Enjoy! It's O.K. to have a little fun. The Lord does not mind you embracing a frolicking spirit, just once in your life. It's your time now.   Reflect!   Use the space below to write your reflective stories.

The Journey To Wholeness & Holiness

The Sasso Bianco, From Val Cordevole[56]

Peaks

---

[56] http://digital.library.upenn.edu/women/edwards/peaks/peaks.html

Peaks Reflections

_____
_____
_____
_____
_____
_____
_____
_____
_____
_____
_____
_____
_____
_____
_____
_____
_____
_____
_____
_____
_____
_____
_____
_____
_____
_____
_____
_____

The Sasso Bianco, From Val Cordevole[57]

Valleys

---

[57] Ibid.

Valleys Reflections

CONTINUING THE

JOURNEY

- C T J -

The journey has only just begun.
This section is **CTJ, "CONTINUING THE JOURNEY."**
First read the **CTJ** Scripture passage then pause to meditate
before expressing ways you plan to continue your journey to
wholeness and holiness. .

- C T J -

If my people, which are called by my name, shall humble themselves, and pray, and seek my face, and turn from their wicked ways; then will I hear from heaven, and will forgive their sin, and will heal their land."

(2 Chronicles 7:14, KJV)

- C T J -

But seek ye first the kingdom of God, and his righteousness; and all these things shall be added unto you. Take therefore no thought for the morrow: for the morrow shall take thought for the things of itself.

(Matthew 6:33-34, KJV)

- C T J -

"Ask, and it shall be given you; seek, and ye shall find; knock, and it shall be opened unto you: For every one that asketh receiveth; and he that seeketh findeth; and to him that knocketh it shall be opened."

(Matthew 7:7-8, KJV)

- C T J -

"If ye abide in me, and my words abide in you, ye shall ask what ye will, and it shall be done unto you. Herein is my Father glorified, that ye bear much fruit; so shall ye be my disciples."

(John 15:7-8, KJV).

- C T J -

"Trust in the LORD with all thine heart; and lean not unto thine own understanding. In all thy ways acknowledge him, and he shall direct thy paths. Be not wise in thine own eyes: fear the LORD, and depart from evil."

(Proverbs 3:5-7, KJV)

- C T J -

"And he shall be like a tree planted by the rivers of water, that bringeth forth his fruit in his season; his leaf also shall not wither; and whatsoever he doeth shall prosper"

(Psalm 1:3, KJV)

- C T J -

"Therefore the ungodly shall not stand in the judgment, nor sinners in the congregation of the righteous"

(Psalm 1:5, KJV)

- C T J -

"For the LORD knoweth the way of the righteous: but the way of the ungodly shall perish."

(Psalm 1:6, KJV)

The Journey To Wholeness & Holiness

Tools For The Journey

Tools For Dealing With Anger
13 Tools

Proverbs 14:29 – He *that is slow to wrath is of great understanding: but he that is hasty of spirit exalteth folly.*

Proverbs 15:1 – *A soft answer turneth away wrath: but grievous words stir up anger.*

Proverbs 22:24-25 – *Make no friendship with an angry man; and with a furious man thou shalt not go Lest thou learn his ways, and get a snare to thy soul.*

Ecclesiastes 7:9 – *Be not hasty in thy spirit to be angry for anger resteth in the bosom of fools.*

Matthew 5:22 – *But I say unto you, That whosoever is angry with his brother without a cause shall be in danger of the judgment: and whosoever shall say to his brother, Raca, shall be in danger of the council: but whosoever shall say Thou fool, shall be in danger of hell fire.*

Galatians 5:19-21 – *Now the works of the flesh are manifest, which are these; Adultery, fornication, uncleanness, lasciviousness, Idolatry, witchcraft, hatred, variance, emulations, wrath, strife, seditions, heresies, Envyings, murders, drunkenness, revellings, and such like: of the which I tell you before as I have also told you in time past that they which do such things shall not inherit the kingdom of God.*

Ephesians 4:26 – *Be ye angry and sin not: let not the sun go down upon your wrath...*

Ephesians 4:31 – *Let all bitterness, and wrath, and anger, and clamour, and evil speaking, be put away from you, with all malice...*

Ephesians 6:4 – *And, ye fathers, provoke not your children to wrath: but bring them up in the nurture and admonition of the Lord.*

Colossians 3:8 – *But now ye also put off all these; anger, wrath, malice, blasphemy, filthy communication out of your mouth.*

1 Timothy 2:8 – *I will therefore that men pray every where, lifting up holy hands, without wrath and doubting.*

Titus 1:7 – *For a bishop must be blameless, as the steward of God; not selfwilled, not soon angry, not given to wine, no striker, not given to filthy lucre...*

James 1:19-20 – *Wherefore, my beloved brethren, let every man be swift to hear slow to speak slow to wrath: For the wrath of man worketh not the righteousness of God.*

Tools for Dealing
With Anxiety
7 Tools

Proverbs 3:24 – *When thou liest down thou shalt not be afraid yea, thou shalt lie down and thy sleep shall be sweet.*

Matthew 6:25-34 – *Therefore I say unto you, Take no thought for your life, what ye shall eat or what ye shall drink nor yet for your body, what ye shall put on Is not the life more than meat, and the body than raiment? Behold the fowls of the air: for they sow not, neither do they reap nor gather into barns; yet your heavenly Father feedeth them. Are ye not much better than they? Which of you by taking thought can add one cubit unto his stature? And why take ye thought for raiment? Consider the lilies of the field, how they grow they toil not, neither do they spin And yet I say unto you, That even Solomon in all his glory was not arrayed like one of these. Wherefore, if God so clothe the grass of the field, which to day is and to morrow is cast into the oven, shall he not much more clothe you, O ye of little faith? Therefore take no thought saying What shall we eat or, What shall we drink or, Wherewithal shall we be clothed (For after all these things do the Gentiles seek) for your heavenly Father knoweth that ye have need of all these things. But seek ye first the kingdom of God, and his righteousness; and all these things shall be added unto you. Take therefore no thought for the morrow: for the morrow shall take thought for the things of itself. Sufficient unto the day is the evil thereof.*

John 14:1 – *Let not your heart be troubled ye believe in God, believe also in me.*

John 14:27 – *Peace I leave with you, my peace I give unto you: not as the world giveth give I unto you. Let not your heart be troubled neither let it be afraid.*

Philippians 4:6-7 – *Be careful for nothing; but in every thing by prayer and supplication with thanksgiving let your requests be made known unto God. And the peace of God, which passeth all understanding, shall keep your hearts and minds through Christ Jesus.*

Colossians 3:15 – *And let the peace of God rule in your hearts, to the which also ye are called in one body; and be ye thankful.*

1 Peter 5:7 – Casting all your care upon him; for he careth for you.

Tools for Dealing With Unforgiveness 6 Tools

Matthew 6:12 – *And forgive us our debts, as we forgive our debtors.*

Matthew 7:1-5 – *Judge not, that ye be not judged. For with what judgment ye judge ye shall be judged and with what measure ye mete it shall be measured to you again And why beholdest thou the mote that is in thy brother's eye, but considerest not the beam that is in thine own eye? Or how wilt thou say to thy brother, Let me pull out the mote out of thine eye; and, behold a beam is in thine own eye? Thou hypocrite, first cast out the beam out of thine own eye; and then shalt thou see clearly to cast out the mote out of thy brother's eye.*

Matthew 18:32-35 – *Then his lord, after that he had called him, said unto him, O thou wicked servant, I forgave thee all that debt, because thou desiredst me: Shouldest not thou also have had compassion on thy fellowservant, even as I had pity on thee? And his lord was wroth and delivered him to the tormentors, till he should pay all that was due unto him. So likewise shall my heavenly Father do also unto you, if ye from your hearts forgive not every one his brother their trespasses.*

Ephesians 4:29-32 – *Let no corrupt communication proceed out of your mouth, but that which is good to the use of edifying, that it may minister grace unto the hearers And grieve not the holy Spirit of God, whereby ye are sealed unto the day of redemption. Let all bitterness, and wrath, and anger, and clamour, and evil speaking, be put away from you,* *with all malice: And be ye kind one to another, tenderhearted, forgiving one another, even as God for Christ's sake hath forgiven you.*

Colossians 3:12-13 – *Put on therefore, as the elect of God, holy and beloved bowels of mercies, kindness, humbleness of mind, meekness, longsuffering; Forbearing one another, and forgiving one another, if any man have a quarrel against any: even as Christ forgave you, so also do ye.*

James 5:9 – *Grudge not one against another, brethren, lest ye be condemned behold the judge standeth before the door.*

Tools For Dealing With The Tongue
9 Tools

Proverbs 10:19 – *In the multitude of words there wanteth not sin: but he that refraineth his lips is wise.*

Proverbs 12:18 – *There is that speaketh like the piercings of a sword: but the tongue of the wise is health.*

Proverbs 17:28 – *Even a fool, when he holdeth his peace is counted wise: and he that shutteth his lips is esteemed a man of understanding.*

Proverbs 21:23 – *Whoso keepeth his mouth and his tongue keepeth his soul from troubles.*

Ephesians 4:29-30 – *Let no corrupt communication proceed out of your mouth, but that which is good to the use of edifying, that it may minister grace unto the hearers And grieve not the holy Spirit of God, whereby ye are sealed unto the day of redemption.*

James 1:19-21 – *Wherefore, my beloved brethren, let every man be swift to hear slow to speak slow to wrath: For the wrath of man worketh not the righteousness of God. Wherefore lay apart all filthiness and superfluity of naughtiness, and receive with meekness the engrafted word, which is able to save your souls.*

James 1:26-27 – *If any man among you seem to be religious, and bridleth not his tongue, but deceiveth his own heart, this man's religion is vain. Pure religion and undefiled before*

God and the Father is this, To visit the fatherless and widows in their affliction, and to keep himself unspotted from the world.

James 3:2-8 – *For in many things we offend all. If any man offend not in word, the same is a perfect man, and able also to bridle the whole body. Behold we put bits in the horses'mouths, that they may obey us; and we turn about their whole body. Behold also the ships, which though they be so great, and are driven of fierce winds, yet are they turned about with a very small helm, whithersoever the governor listeth Even so the tongue is a little member, and boasteth great things Behold how great a matter a little fire kindleth And the tongue is a fire, a world of iniquity: so is the tongue among our members, that it defileth the whole body, and setteth on fire the course of nature; and it is set on fire of hell. For every kind of beasts, and of birds, and of serpents, and of things in the sea, is tamed and hath been tamed of mankind: But the tongue can no man tame it is an unruly evil, full of deadly poison.*

James 3:9-14 – *Therewith bless we God, even the Father; and therewith curse we men, which are made after the similitude of God. Out of the same mouth proceedeth blessing and cursing. My brethren, these things ought not so to be. Doth a fountain send forth at the same place sweet water and bitter? Can the fig tree, my brethren, bear olive berries? either a vine, figs? so can no fountain both yield salt water and fresh. Who is a wise man and endued with knowledge among you? let him shew out of a good conversation his works with meekness of wisdom. But if ye have bitter envying and strife in your hearts, glory not, and lie not...*

The Journey To Wholeness & Holiness

THE JOURNEY TO
wholeness
& HOLINESS
FASTING AND PRAYING

ABOUT THE AUTHOR

Robert F. Loggins, Sr., earned his B.S., University of Southern Mississippi, Hattiesburg, Mississippi; then he earned his Masters of Divinity Degree at New Orleans Baptist Theological Seminary; and finally he completed all his core courses for his Doctorate of Ministries Degree at Covenant Theological Seminary, St. Louis, Missouri. He is the Foundering Pastor-Teacher of The WORD Is Alive Ministries, a disciple making church in St. Peters, Missouri. He also serves as the African-American church strategist for the St. Louis Metro Baptist Association in partnership with the Missouri Baptist State Convention and the North American Mission Board (NAMB); he is the Assistant to the Director of Evangelism of the Missionary Baptist State Convention of National Baptist. He has served as a Commissioned Missionary and Church Planter. He writes for the Evangelism Department of the Missionary Baptist State Convention of Nation Baptist. He is known as a gifted Bible expositor and conference speaker (Ponca Bible Camp and other church camps and retreat events). He is a sought after lecturer, revivalist, preacher and teacher. He serves as President of The Robert Loggins, Sr., Ministries, LLC and In The WORD Ministries, which are outreach teaching and equipping ministries of The In The WORD Ministries. He is also the President of The Christian Life School of Theology and Discipleship. He and his wife, Cassandra has two awesome sons, Robert, Jr., and Jordan Mathia. He and his wife are also very proud grandparents to their first grandchild, a beautiful little lady, Madison, the daughter of Robert and Christy Loggins, Jr., of Birmingham, Alabama.

The Journey to

wholeness
& HOLINESS

Fasting and Praying

For More Information
About How To Obtain More Copies Of
The Journey To Wholeness & Holiness

Write:

The WORD Is Alive Ministries
a disciple making church
Pastor Robert F. Loggins, Sr.
P. O. Box 1175
St. Peters, MO 63376

Call:

(636) 938-6400

Visit:

Our Website & Click
On The Pastor's Page
To Purchase Additional Copies Of

The Journey To Wholeness & Holiness
WWW.TWIAM.ORG

The WORD Is Alive Ministries, a disciple making church
Where Love Is The Most Excellent Way!
The Great Commission – GO – Matthew 28:18-20
The Greatest Commandment – LOVE – Matthew 22:37-40

GO LOVE

THE JOURNEY TO

wholeness
& HOLINESS

FASTING AND PRAYING

The Journey To Wholeness & Holiness

Basic Bible Teaching Series
The Christian Family Series: Teaching Lesson 1

For Husbands Only!!!
A Wise WORD To Husbands About Their Wives

The Secret Of A Happy Home
Part 1: Beyond The Physical

BY
Pastor Robert F. Loggins, Sr.

*Does your husband need help in understanding what
your real needs are as his wife?
Would you like to see God do a new thing in your marriage?
What does it take for a godly Christian man to move
"Beyond The Physical" to "The Spiritual" with his wife?
Is it possible to achieve God's Standard of Marital Happiness!*

Featured Books In The Family Series
Lesson 1 – For Husbands Only – available now
Lesson 2 – For Wives Only – coming soon.
Lesson 3 – For Children Only – coming soon.

Contact:
The WORD Is Alive Ministries
P. O. Box 1175
St. Peters, MO 63376

The Journey To Wholeness & Holiness